FOR ORGANS, PIANOS & ELECTRONIC KEYBOARDS

2ND EDITION

E-Z PLAY TODAY

115

THE GREATEST WALTZES

ISBN 978-1-4234-4402-2

HAL•LEONARD®
CORPORATION

7777 W. BLUEMOUND RD. P.O. BOX 13819 MILWAUKEE, WI 53213

Visit Hal Leonard Online at
www.halleonard.com

CONTENTS

Alice Blue Gown

from IRENE

Registration 4
Rhythm: Waltz

Lyric by Joseph McCarthy
Music by Harry Tierney

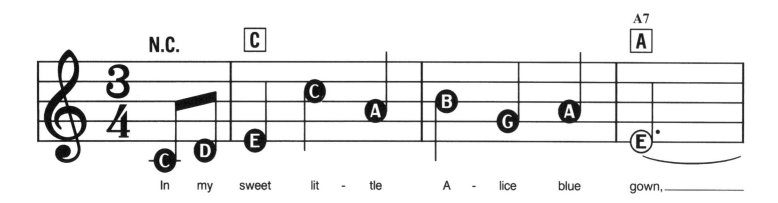

In my sweet lit - tle A - lice blue gown,____

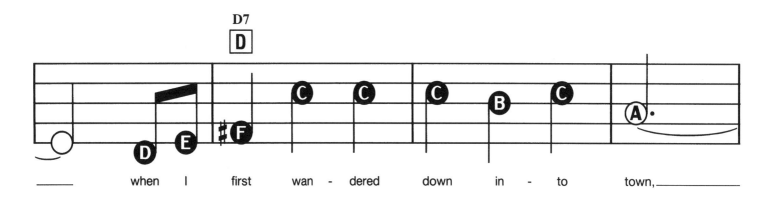

____ when I first wan - dered down in - to town,____

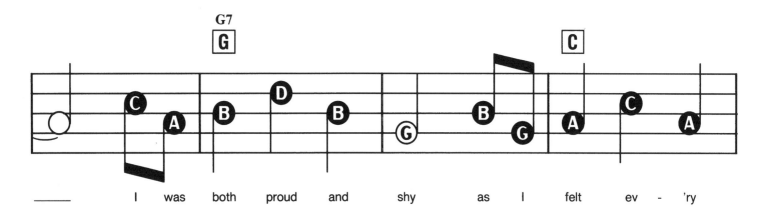

____ I was both proud and shy as I felt ev - 'ry

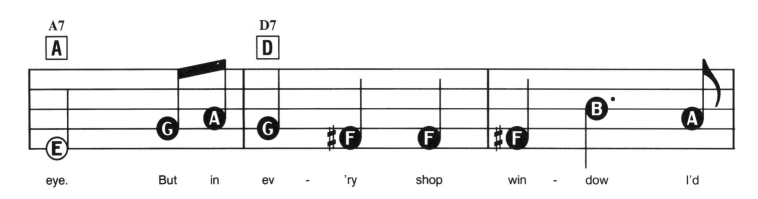

eye. But in ev - 'ry shop win - dow I'd

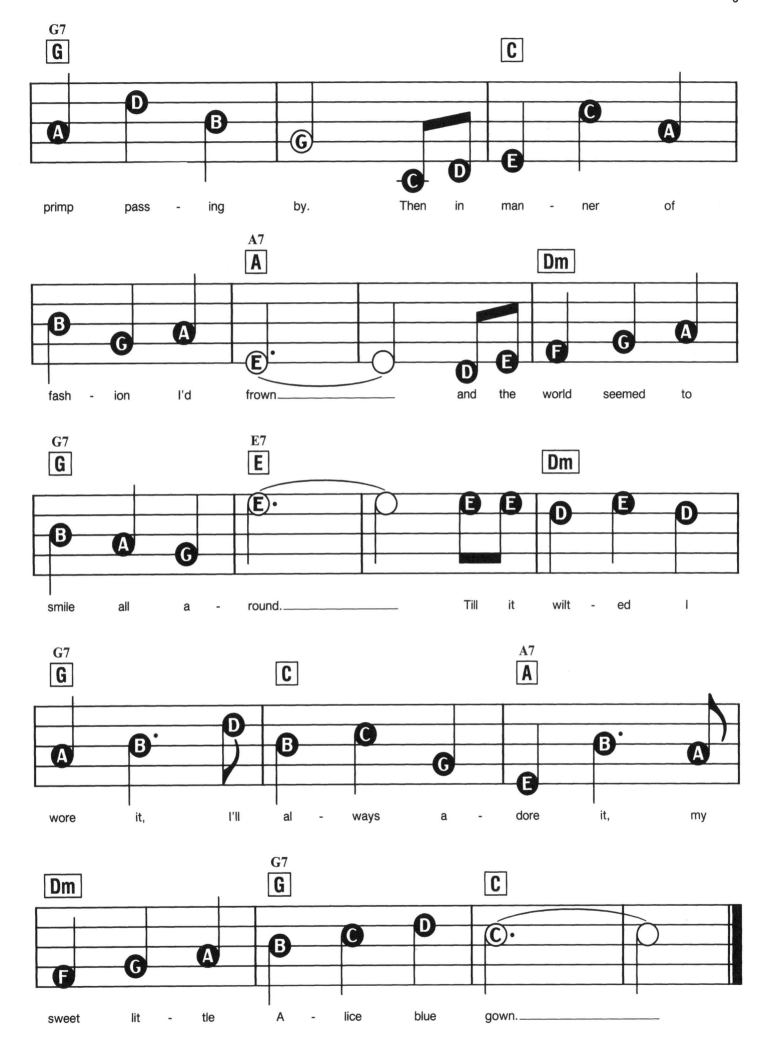

Allegheny Moon

Registration 9
Rhythm: Waltz

Words and Music by Dick Manning
and Al Hoffman

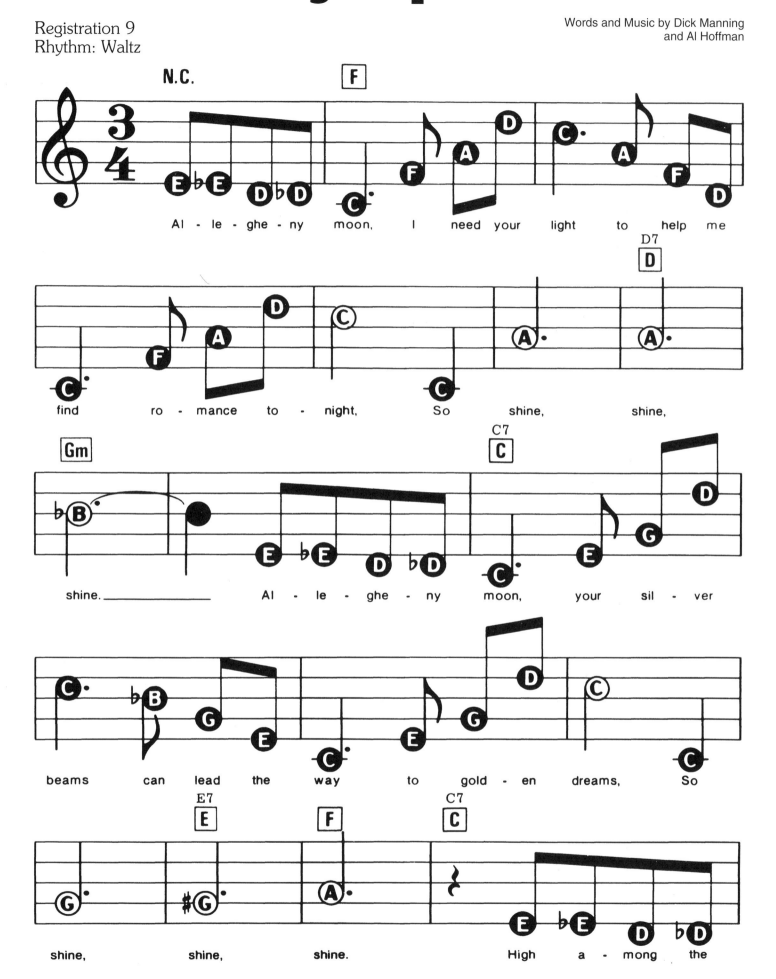

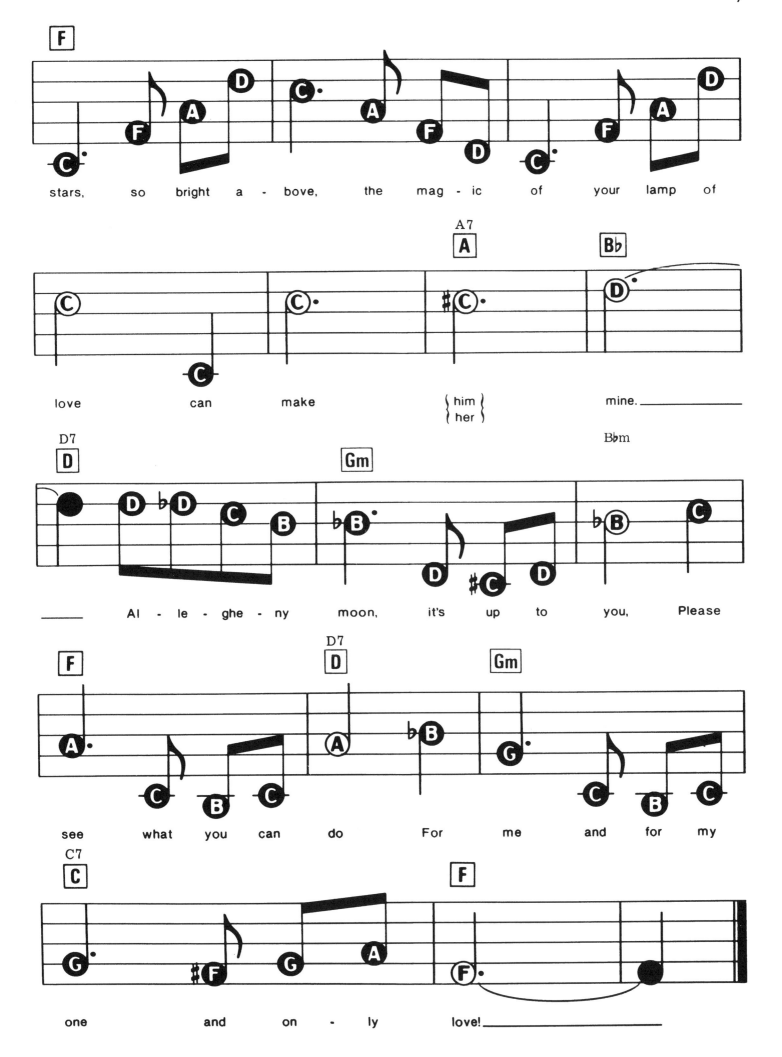

Anniversary Song
from the Columbia Picture THE JOLSON STORY

Registration 4
Rhythm: Waltz

By Al Jolson and
Saul Chaplin

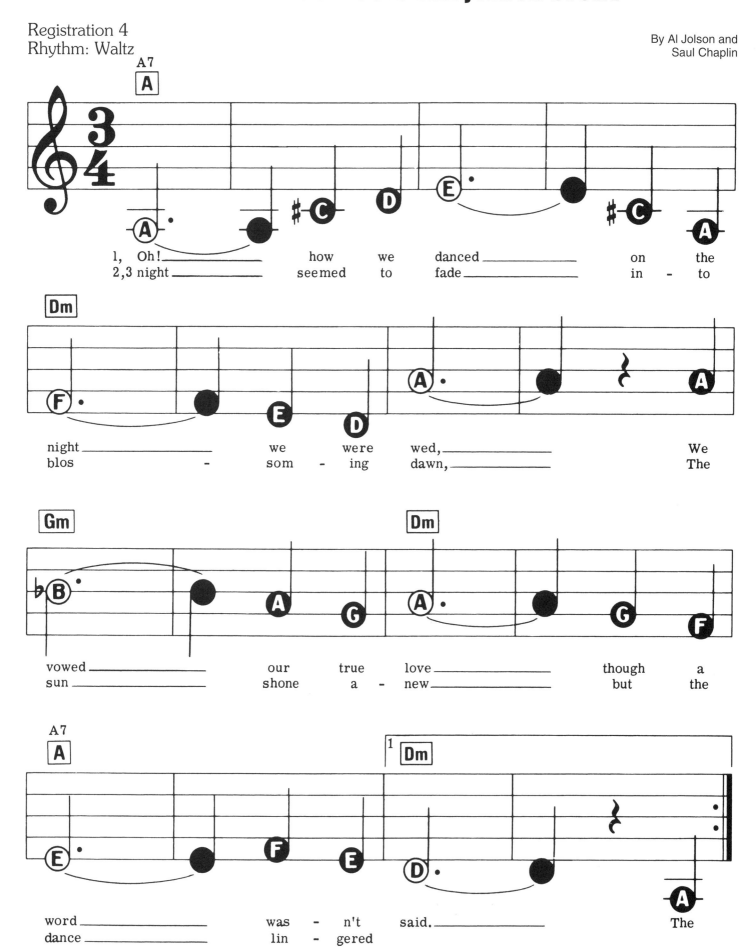

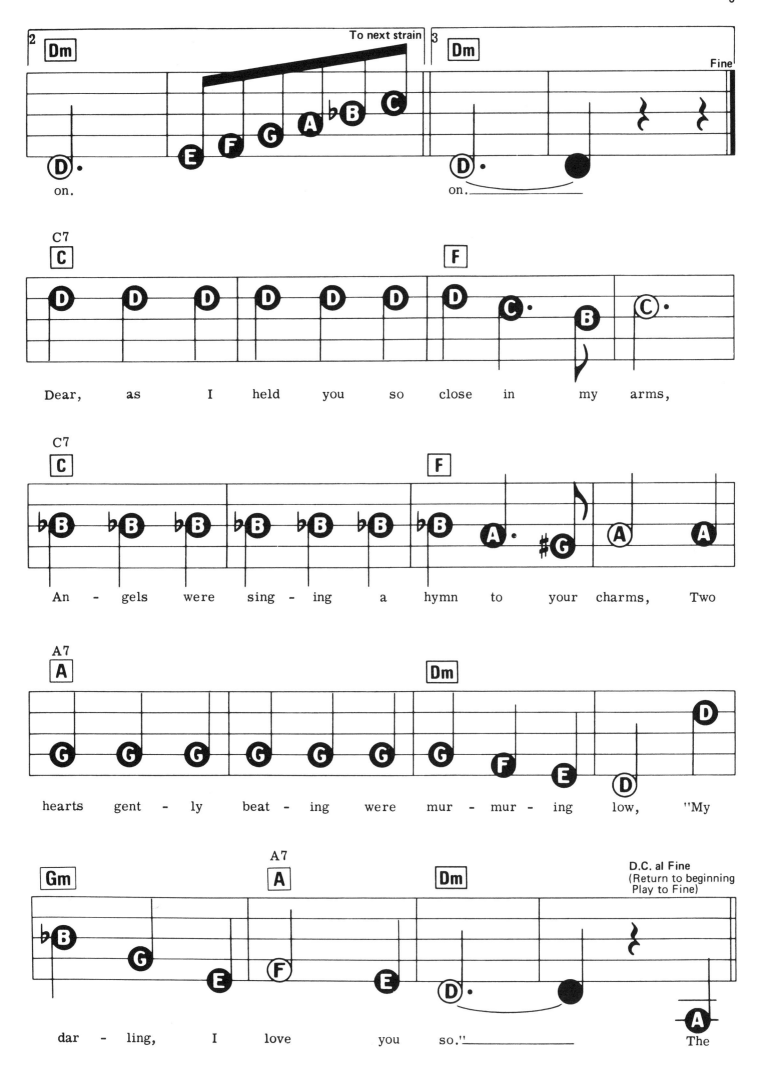

The Anniversary Waltz

Registration 3
Rhythm: Waltz

Words and Music by Al Dubin
and Dave Franklin

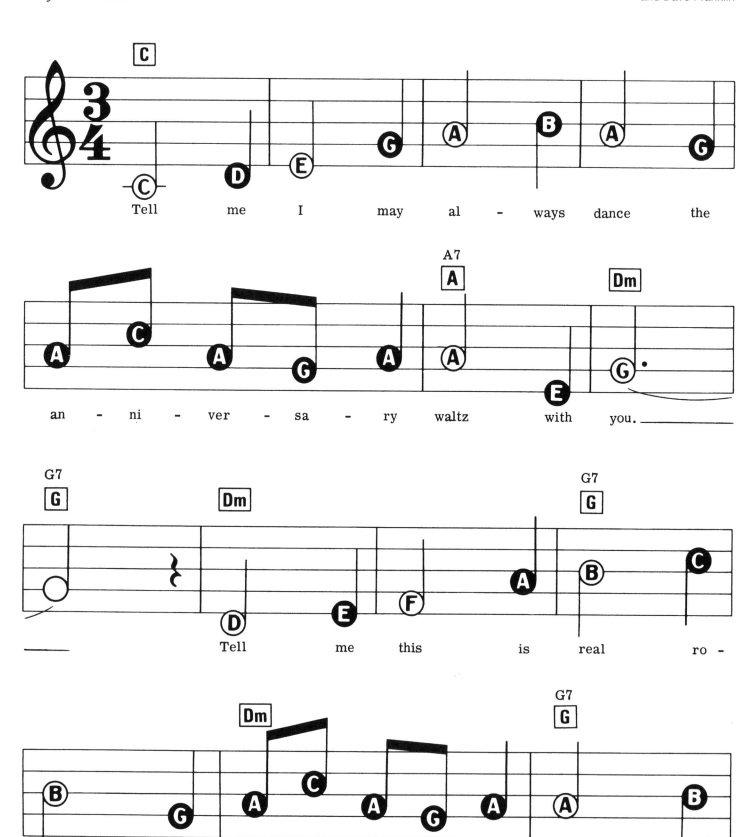

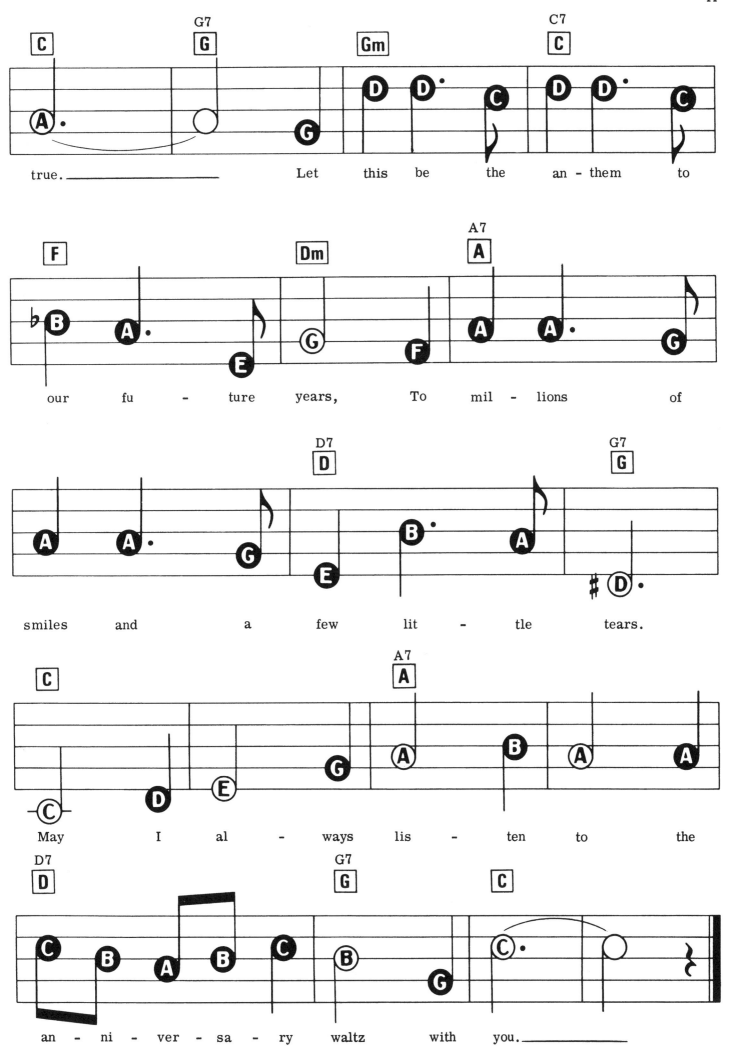

Are You Lonesome Tonight?

Registration 1
Rhythm: Waltz

Words and Music by Roy Turk
and Lou Handman

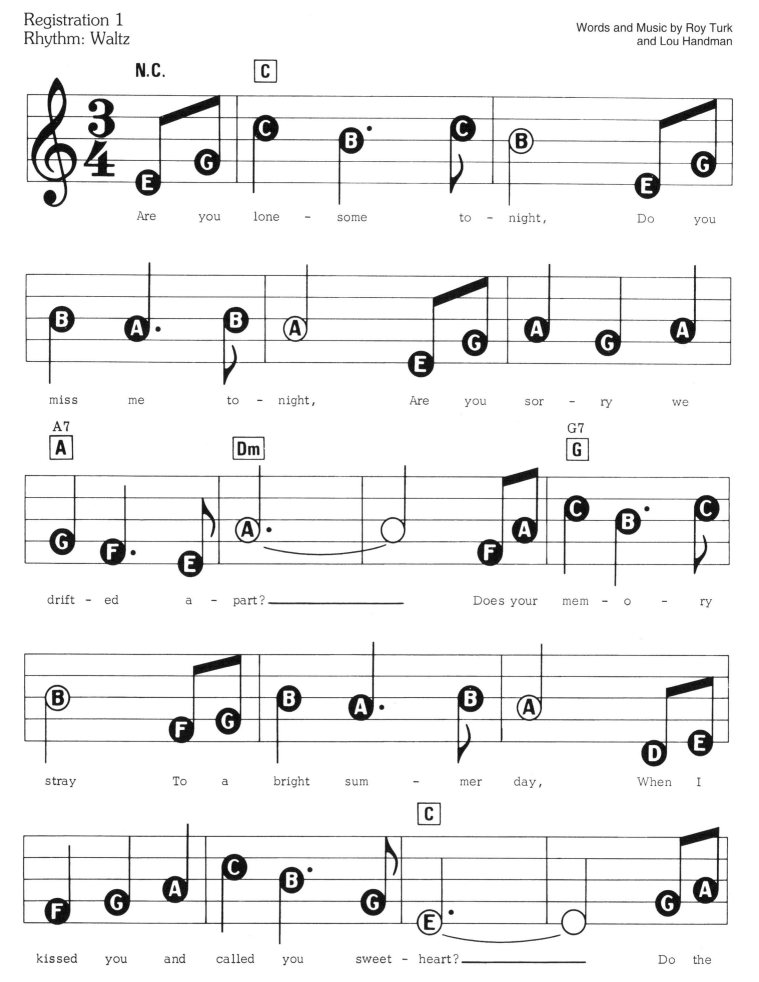

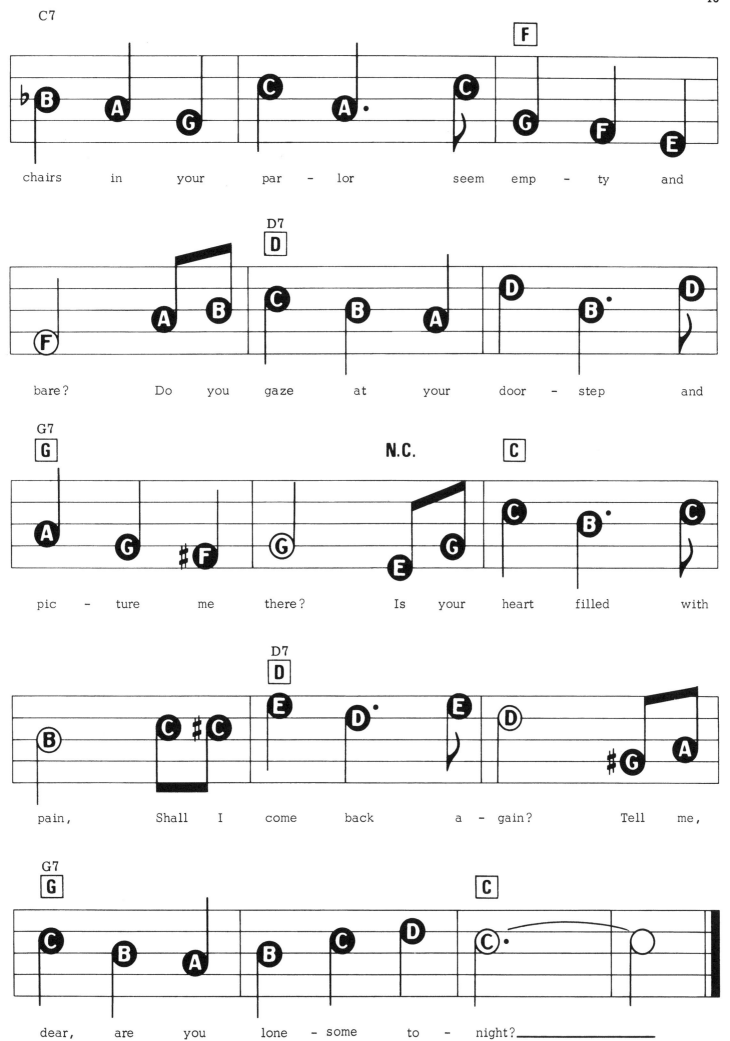

The Blue Skirt Waltz

Registration 2
Rhythm: Waltz

Words by Mitchell Parish
Music by Vaclav Blaha

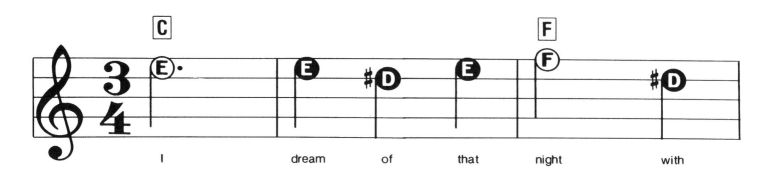

I   dream of   that   night   with

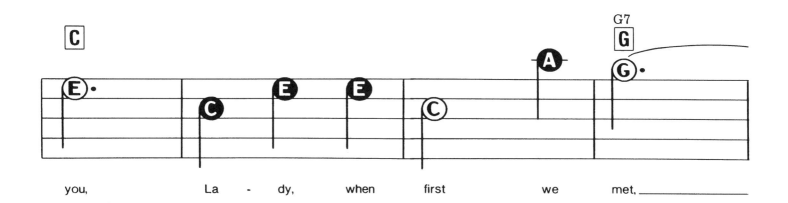

you,   La - dy,   when   first   we   met,_____

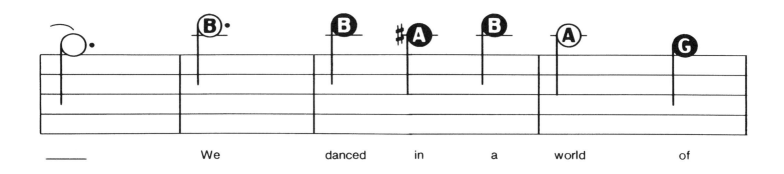

_____   We   danced   in   a   world   of

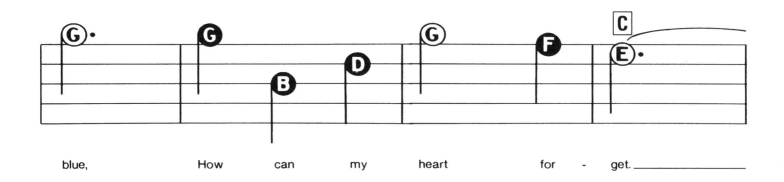

blue,   How   can   my   heart   for - get._____

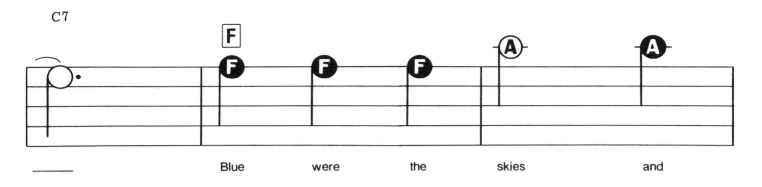

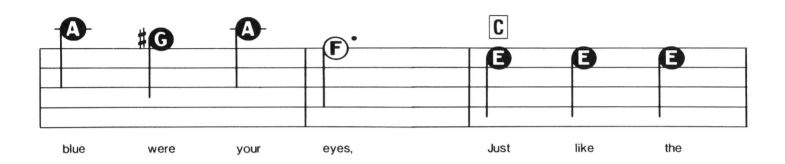

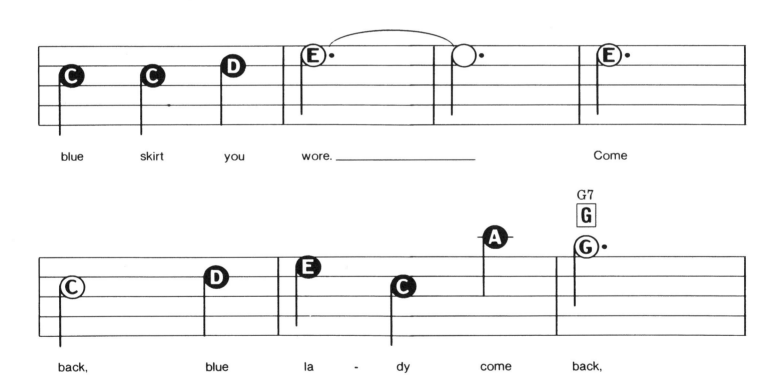

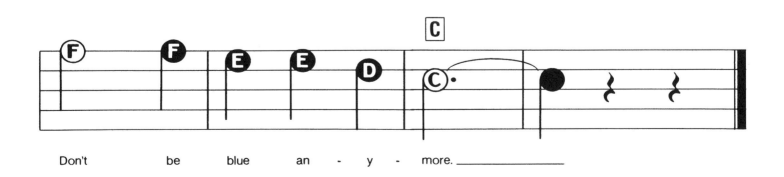

Cara, mia

Registration 3
Rhythm: Waltz

By Julio Trapani
and Lee Lange

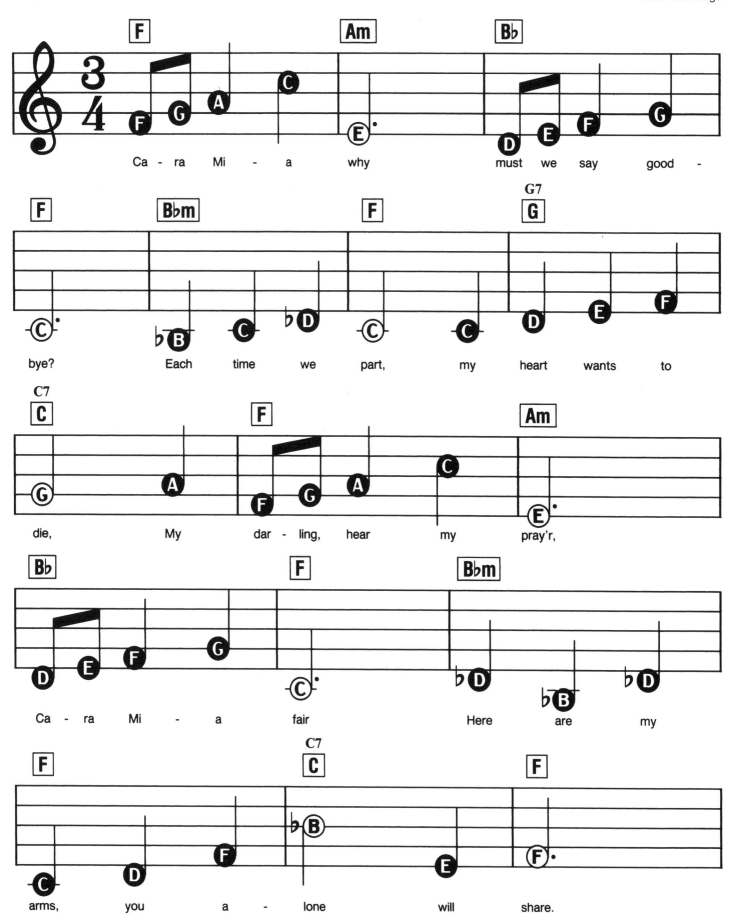

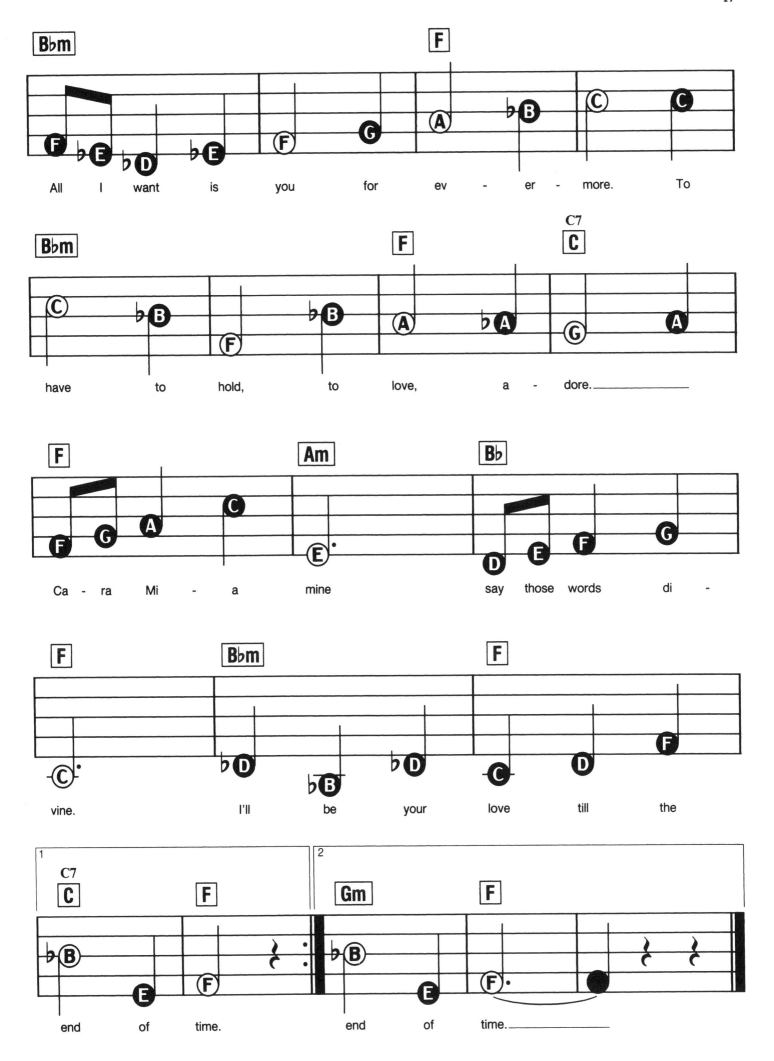

Carolina Moon

Registration 3
Rhythm: Waltz

Lyric by Benny Davis
Music by Joe Burke

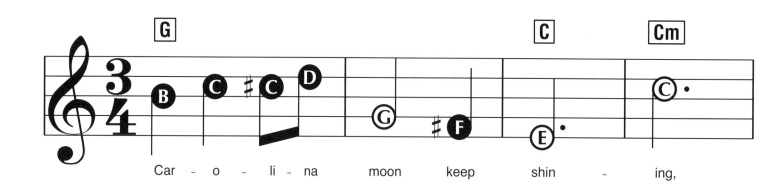

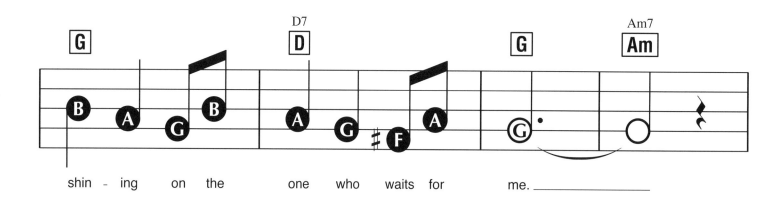

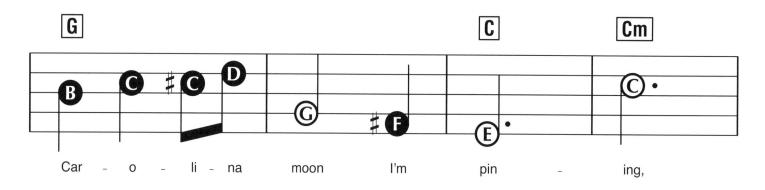

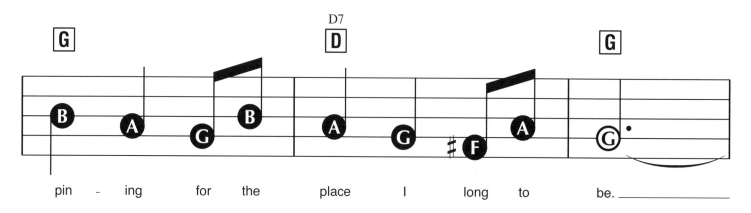

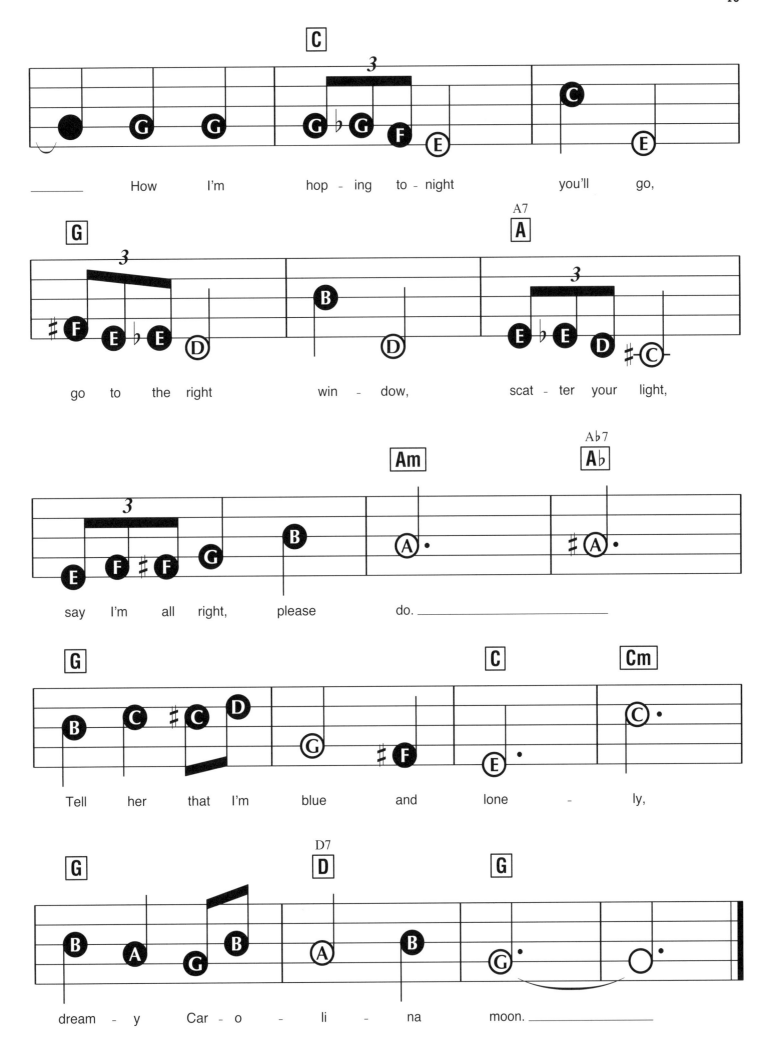

I Wonder Who's Kissing Her Now

Registration 1
Rhythm: Waltz

Lyrics by Will M. Hough and Frank R. Adams
Music by Joseph E. Howard and Harold Orlob

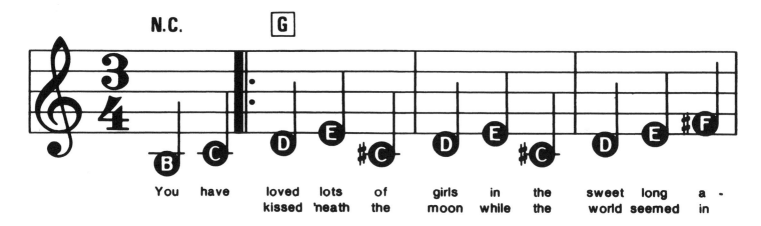

You have loved lots of girls in the sweet long a-
kissed 'neath the moon while the world seemed in

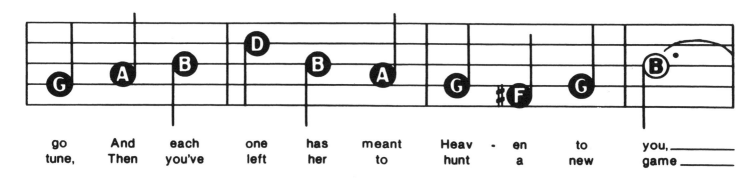

go And each one has meant Heav - en to you, _____
tune, Then you've left her to hunt a new game _____

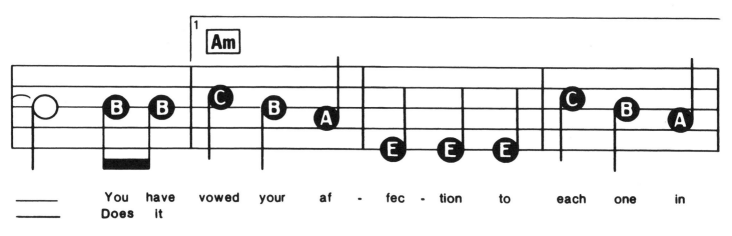

_____ You have vowed your af - fec - tion to each one in
_____ Does it

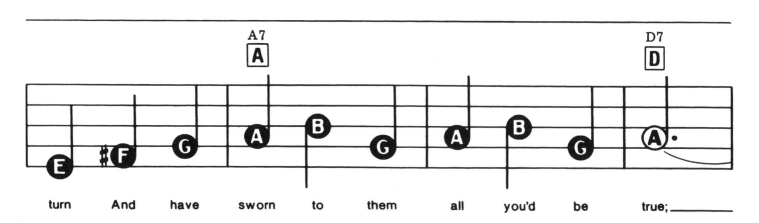

turn And have sworn to them all you'd be true; _____

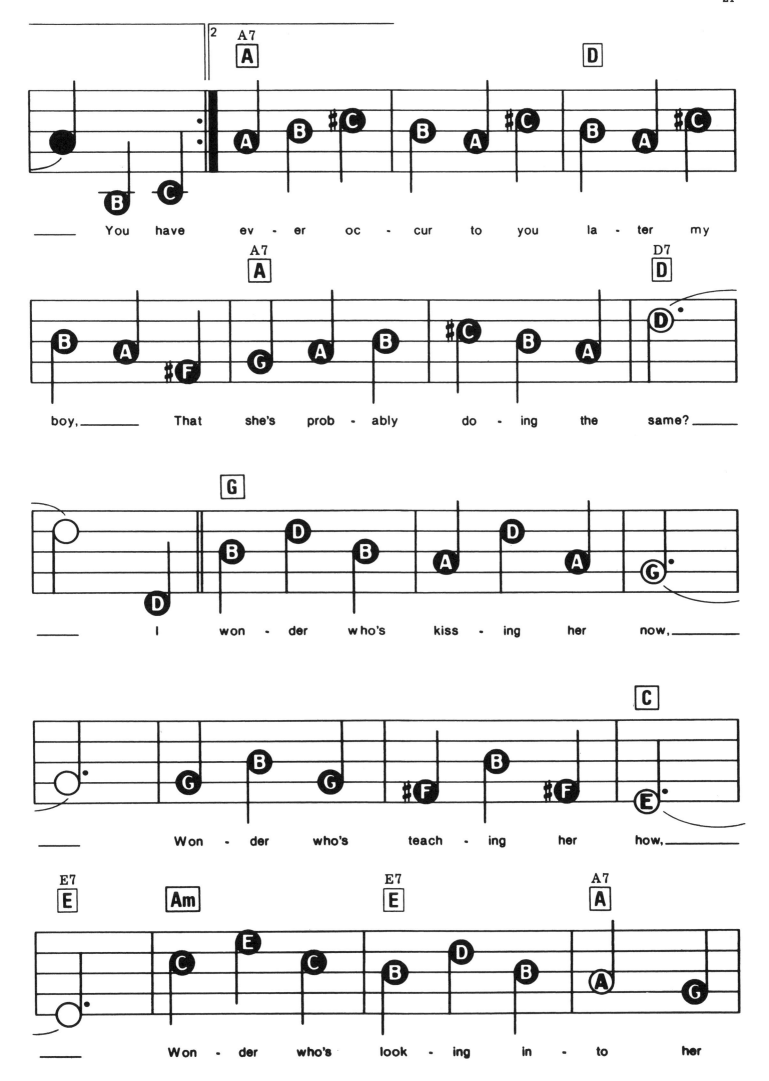

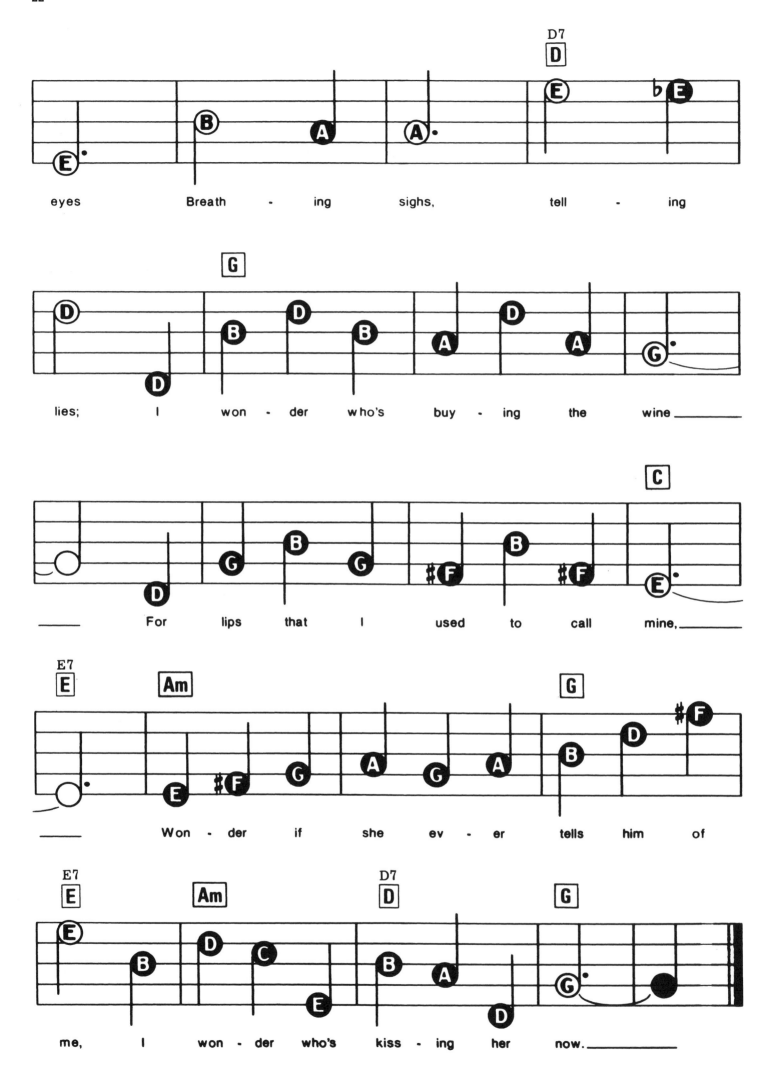

Cuckoo Waltz

Registration 1
Rhythm: Waltz

By Johan Jonasson

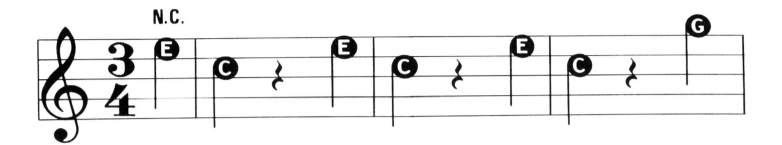

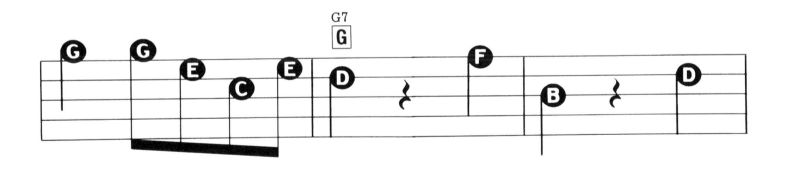

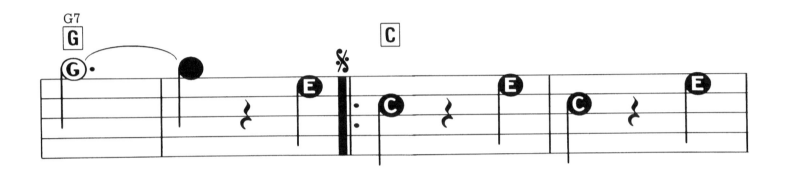

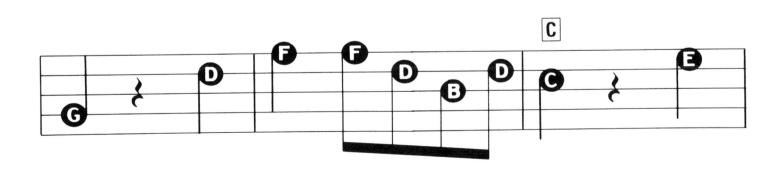

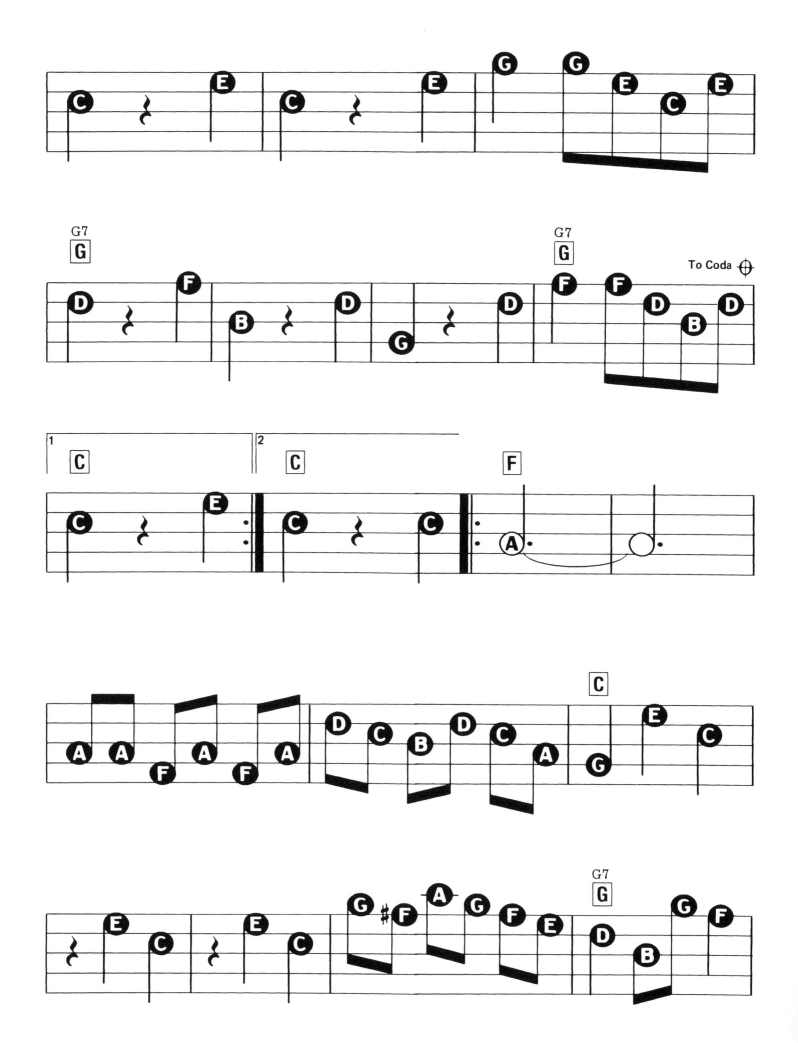

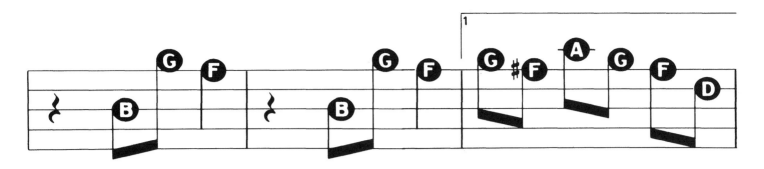

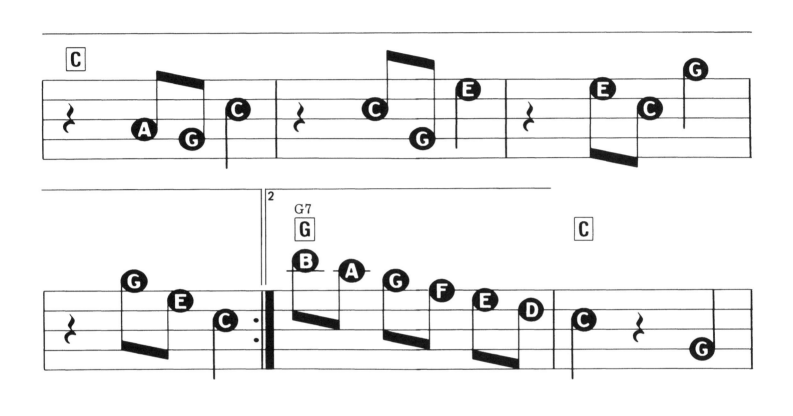

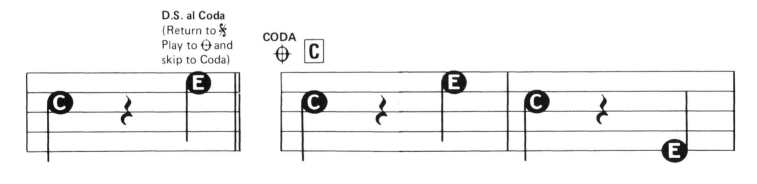

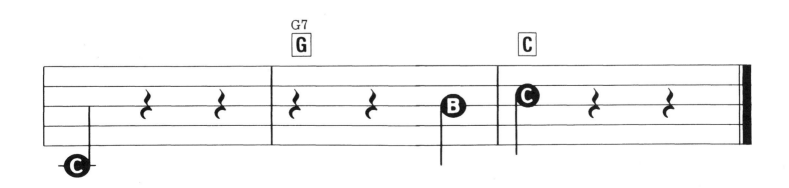

Do I Hear a Waltz?
from DO I HEAR A WALTZ?

Registration 10
Rhythm: Waltz

Music by Richard Rodgers
Lyrics by Stephen Sondheim

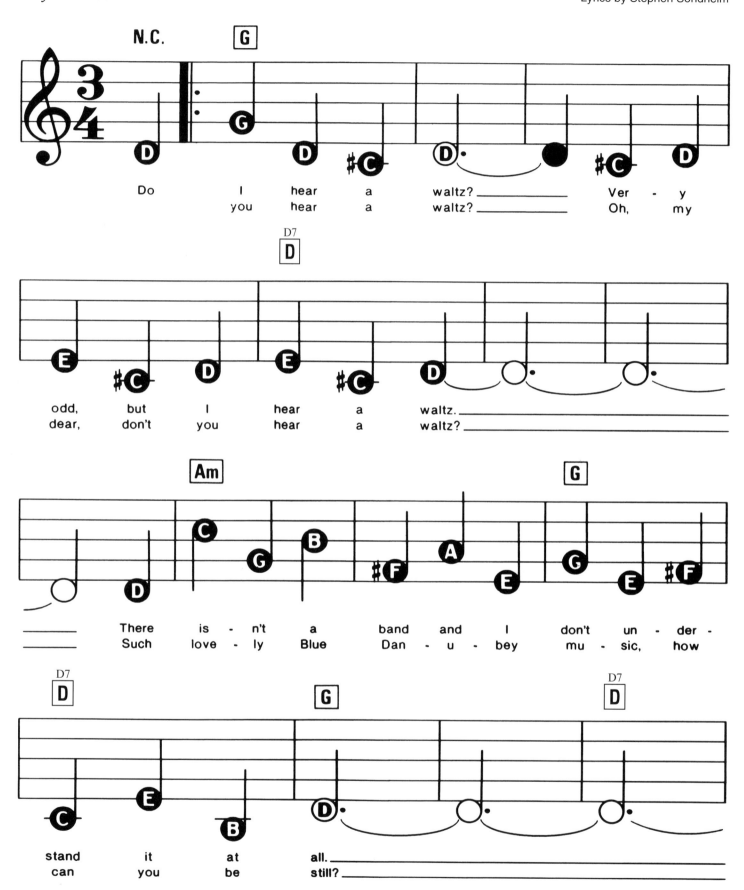

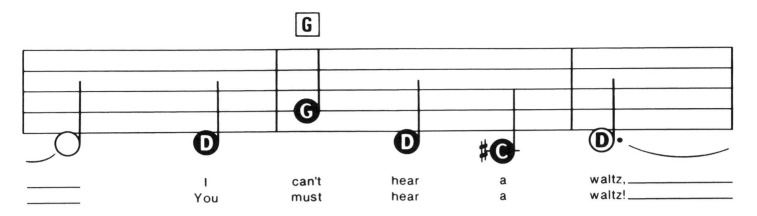

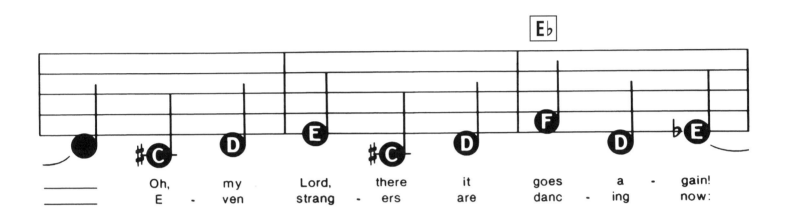

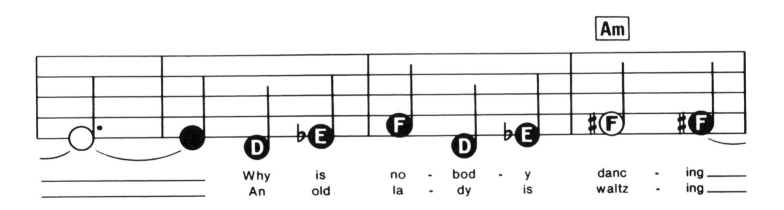

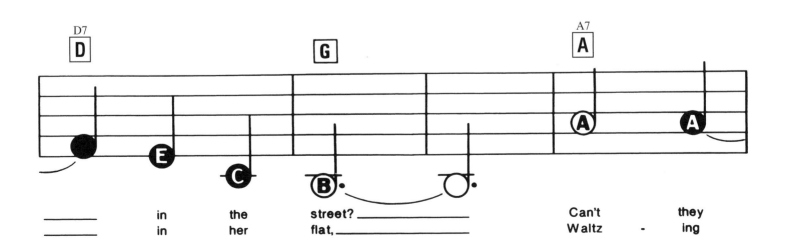

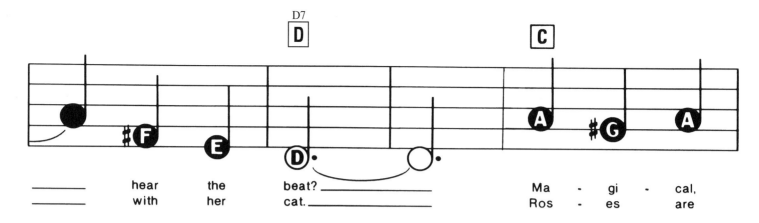

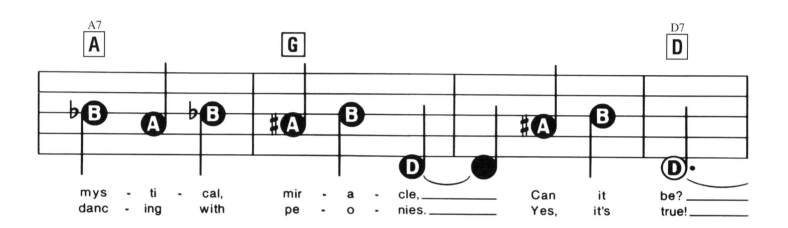

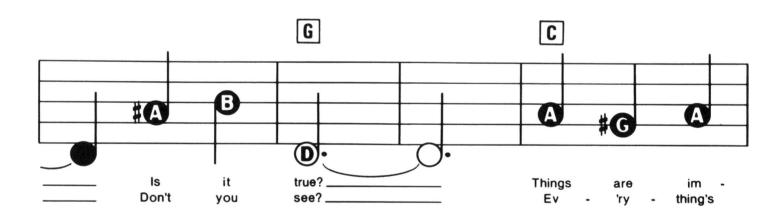

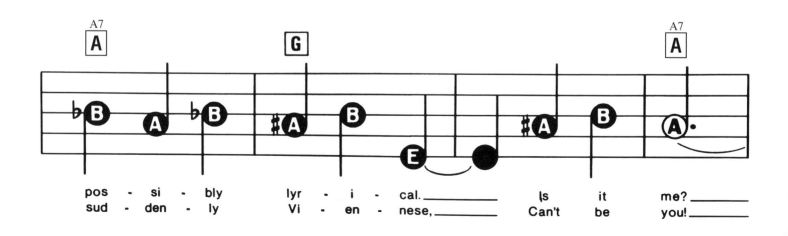

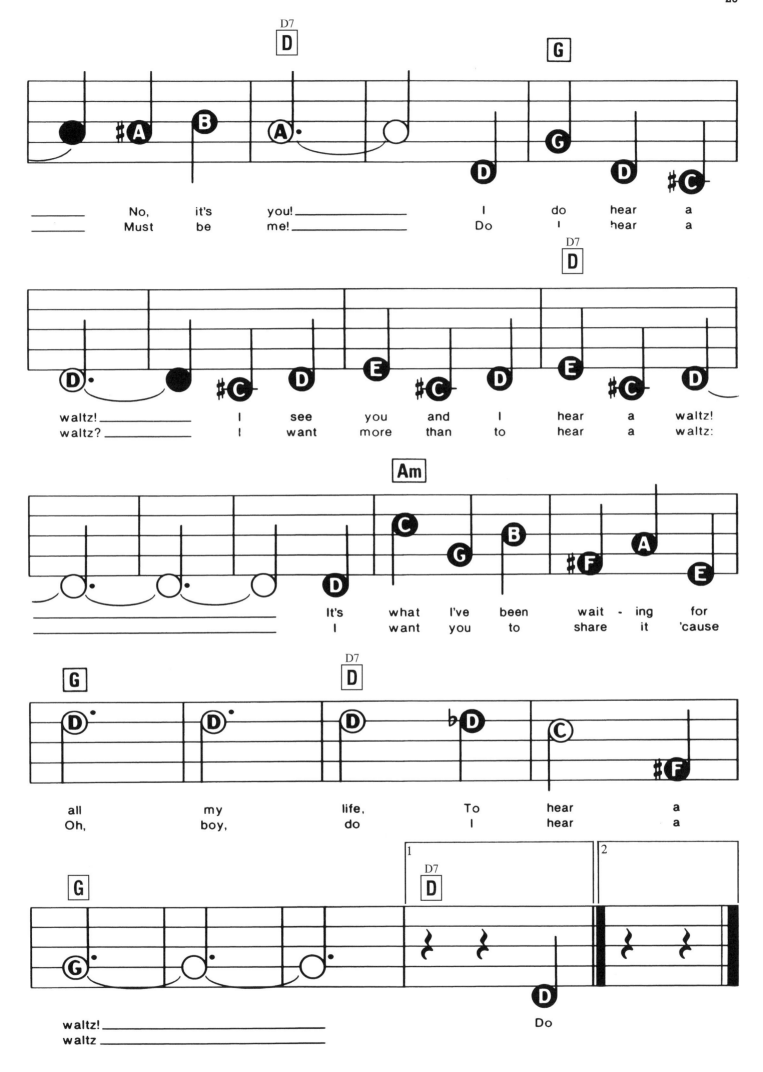

29

Du, du liegst mir im Herzen
(You, You Weigh on My Heart)

Registration 4
Rhythm: Waltz

German Folksong

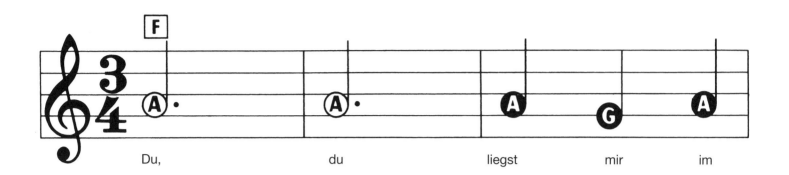

Du,　du　liegst　mir　im

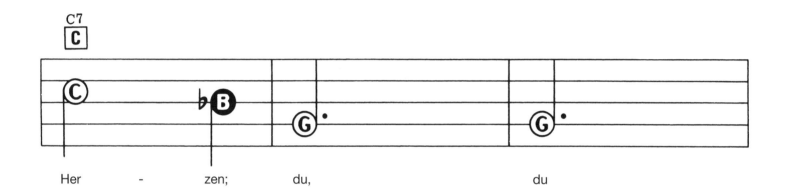

Her - zen;　du,　du

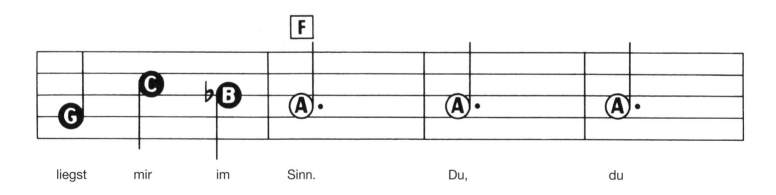

liegst　mir　im　Sinn.　Du,　du

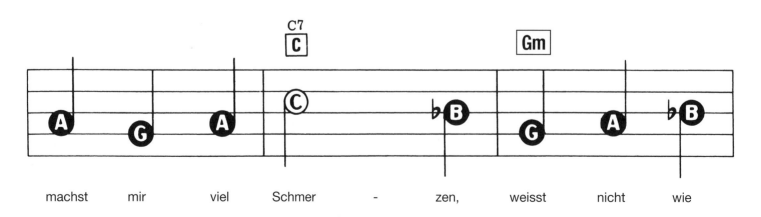

machst　mir　viel　Schmer - zen,　weisst　nicht　wie

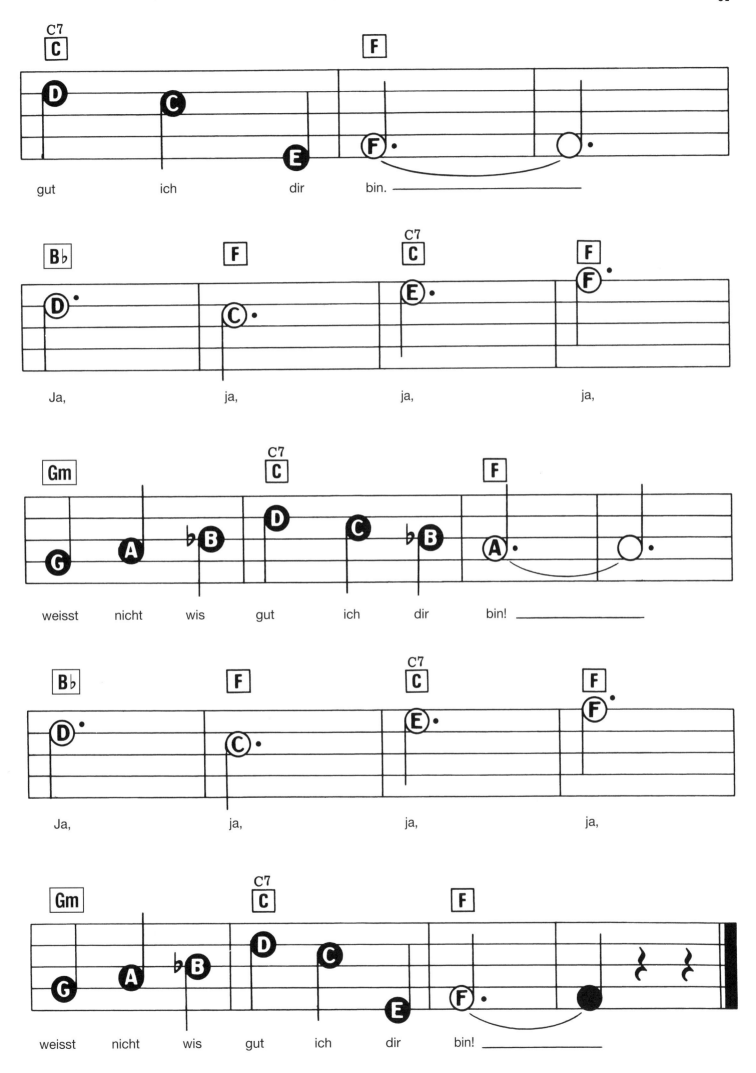

Edelweiss
from THE SOUND OF MUSIC

Registration 4
Rhythm: Waltz

Lyrics by Oscar Hammerstein II
Music by Richard Rodgers

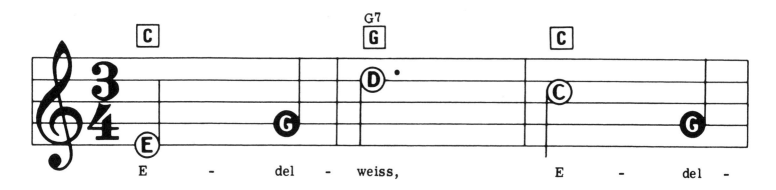

E - del - weiss,   E - del -

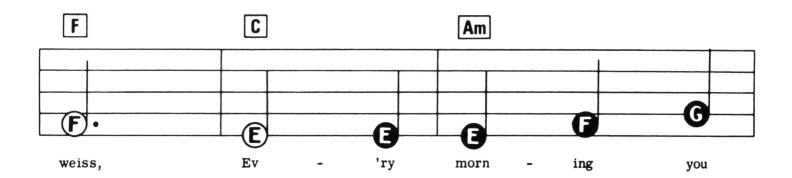

weiss,   Ev - 'ry   morn - ing   you

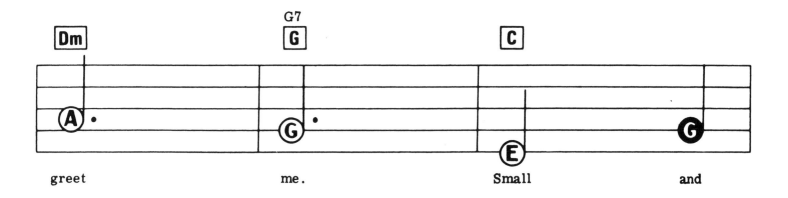

greet   me.   Small   and

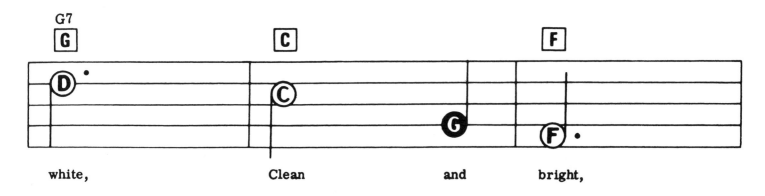

white,   Clean   and   bright,

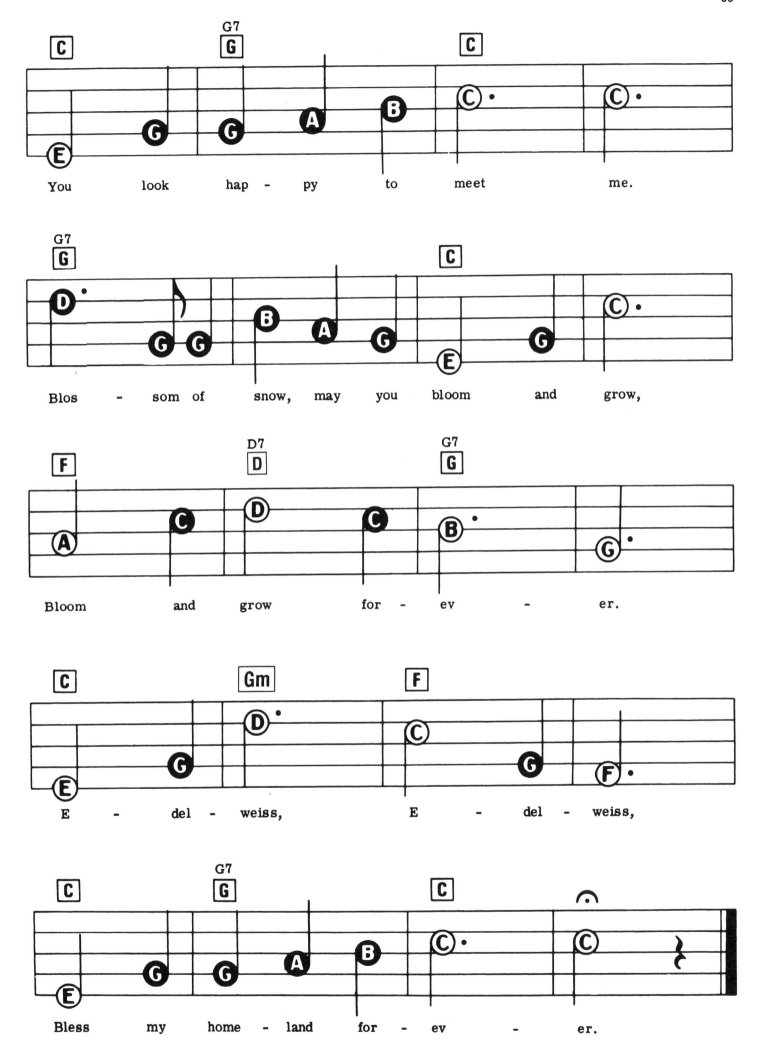

Falling in Love with Love
from THE BOYS FROM SYRACUSE

Registration 5
Rhythm: Waltz

Words by Lorenz Hart
Music by Richard Rodgers

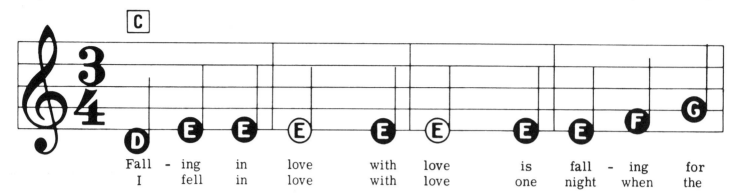

Fall - ing in love with love is fall - ing for
I fell in love with with love is one night when for the

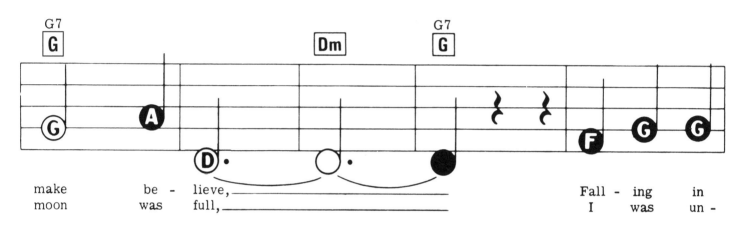

make be - lieve, _____ Fall - ing in
moon was full, _____ I was un -

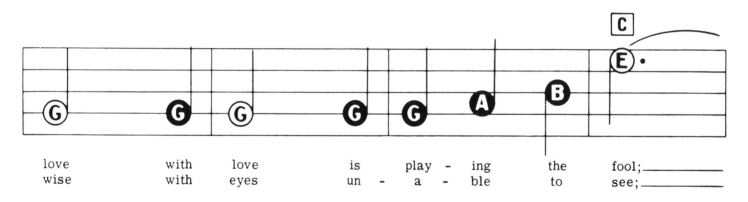

love with love is play - ing the fool; _____
wise with eyes un - a - ble to see; _____

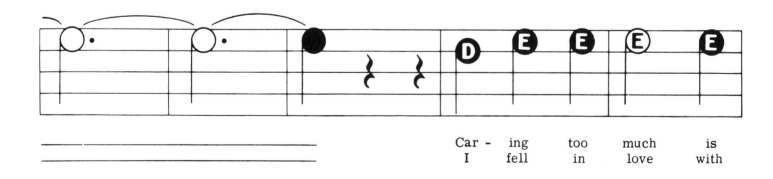

_____ Car - ing too much is
I fell in love with

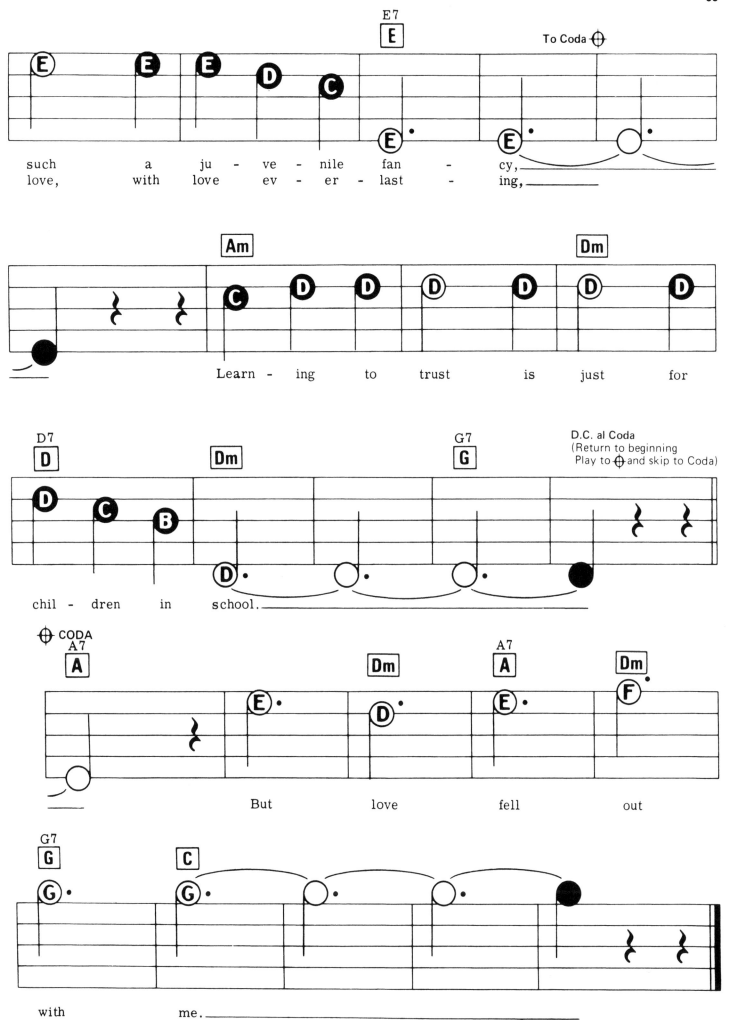

Fascination
(Valse Tzigane)

Registration 10
Rhythm: Waltz

By F.D. Marchetti

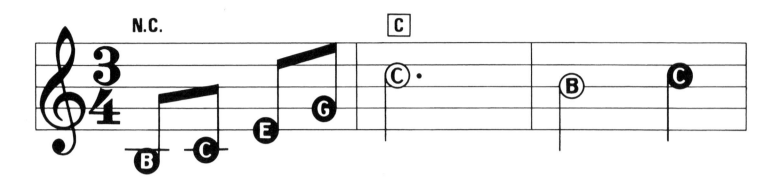

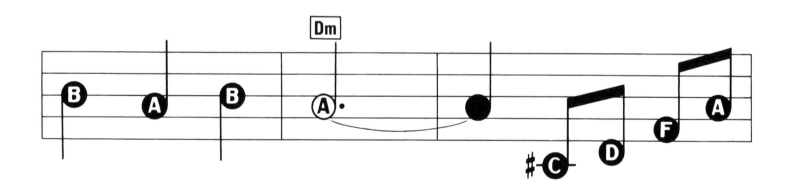

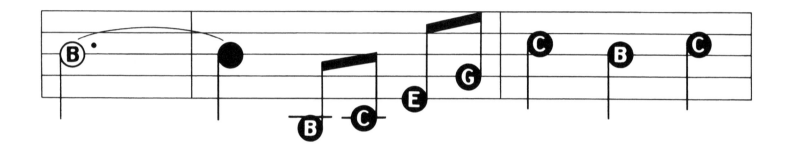

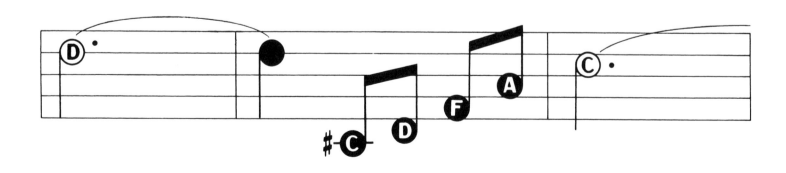

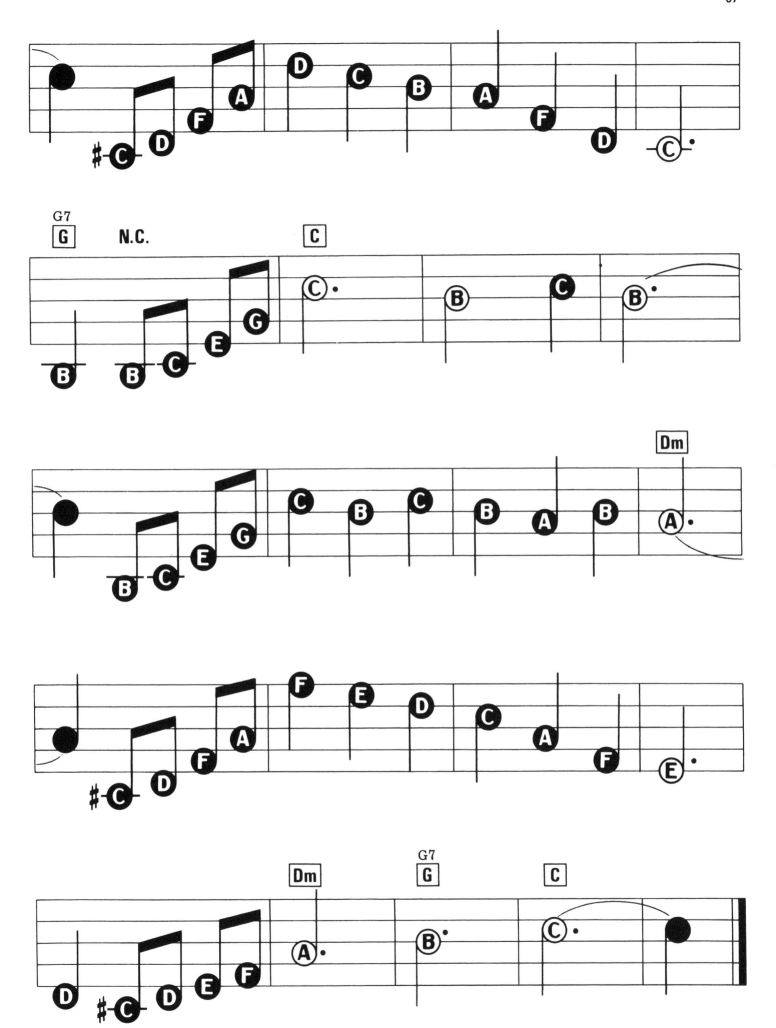

I'll Take Romance

Registration 3
Rhythm: Waltz

Lyrics by Oscar hammerstein II
Music by Ben Oakland

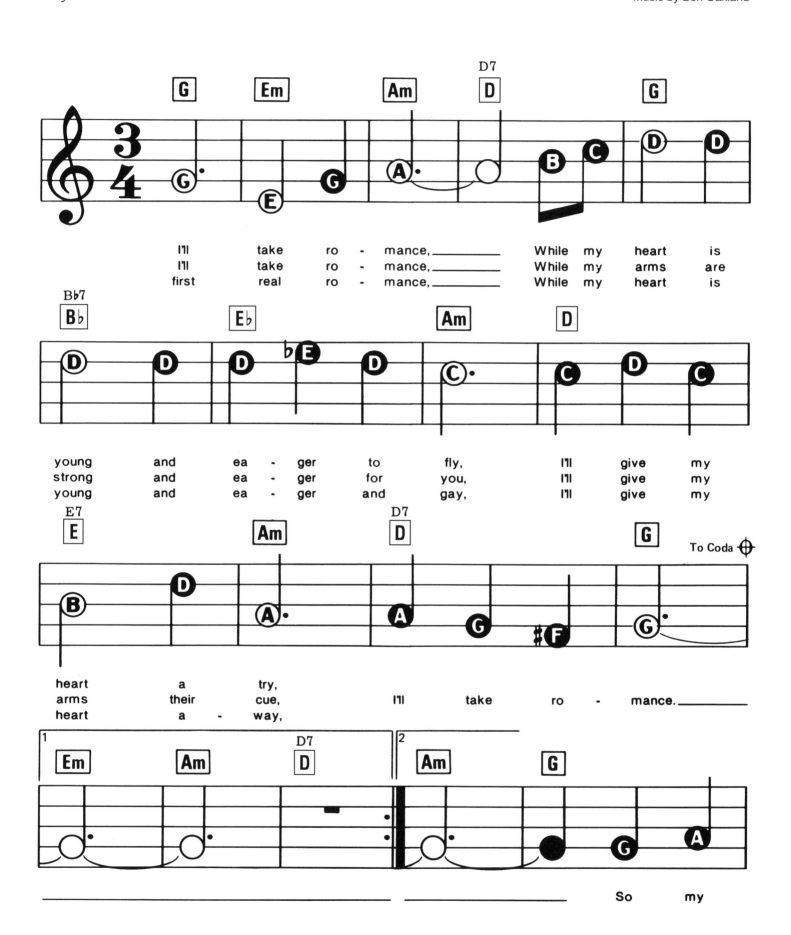

I'll take ro - mance,_____ While my heart is
I'll take ro - mance,_____ While my arms is
first real ro - mance,_____ While my heart is

young and ea - ger to fly, I'll give my
strong and ea - ger for you, I'll give my
young and ea - ger and gay, I'll give my

heart a try,
arms their cue, I'll take ro - mance._____
heart a - way,

So my

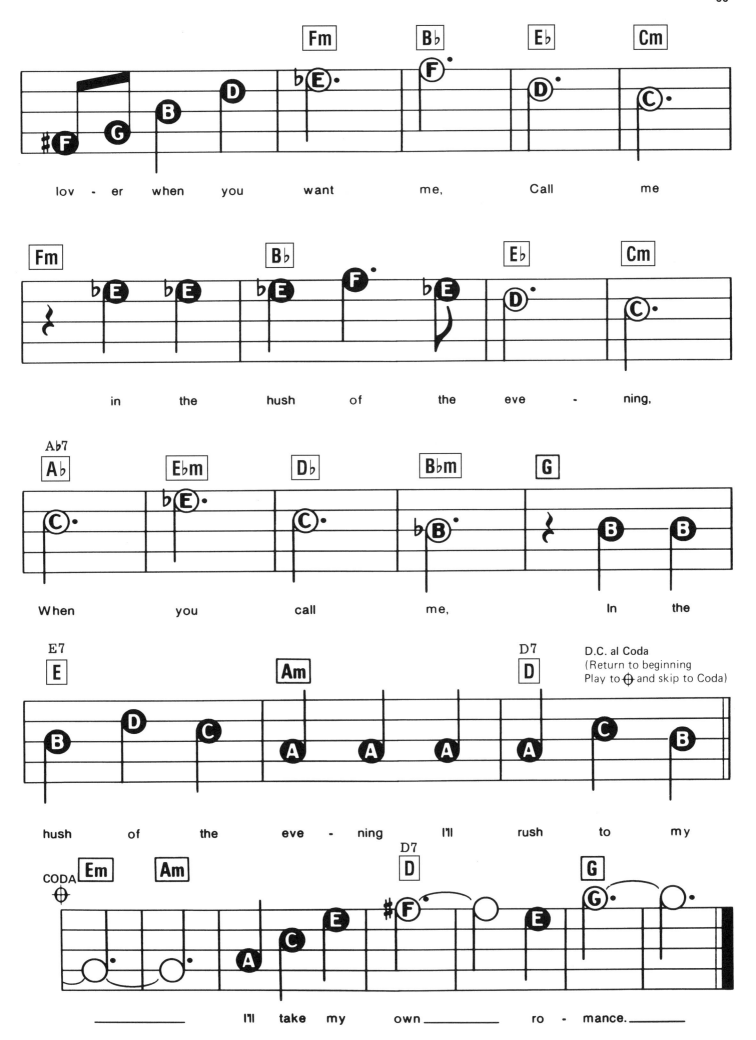

It's a Grand Night for Singing
from STATE FAIR

Registration 5
Rhythm: Waltz

Lyrics by Oscar Hammerstein II
Music by Richard Rodgers

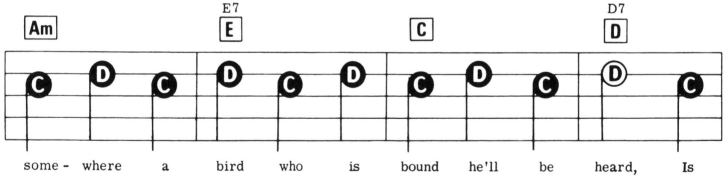

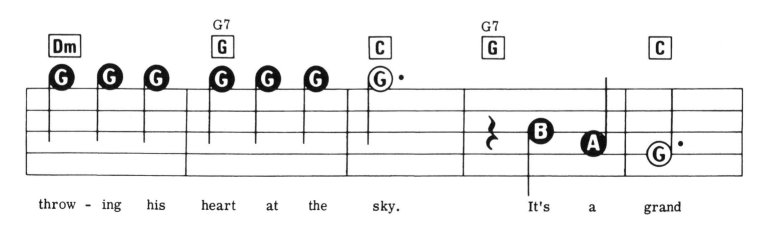

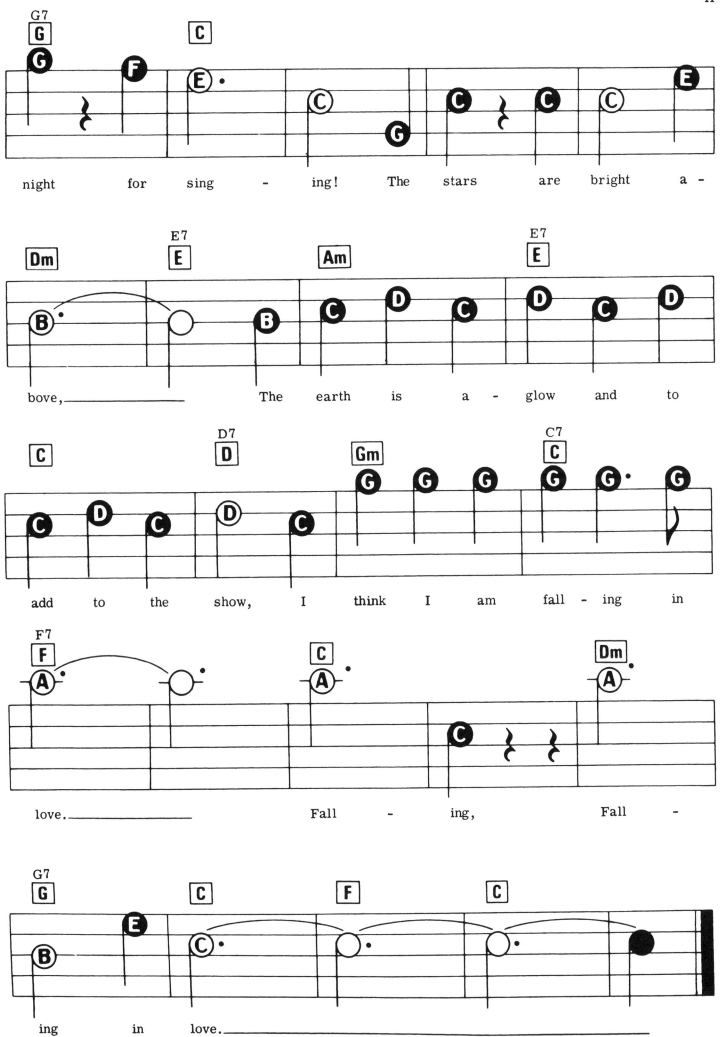

Kentucky Waltz

Registration 4
Rhythm: Waltz

Words and Music by
Bill Monroe

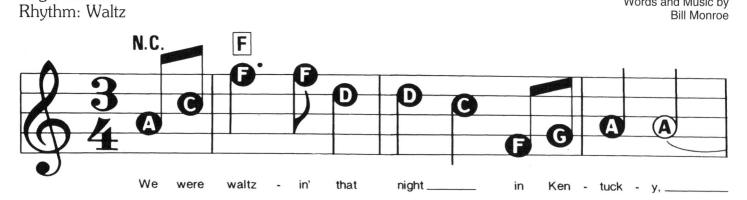

We were waltz - in' that night _____ in Ken - tuck - y, _____

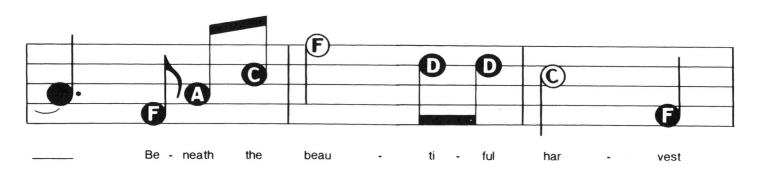

_____ Be - neath the beau - ti - ful har - vest

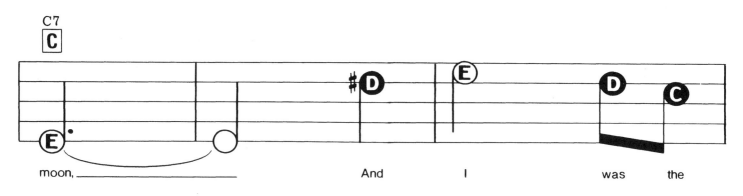

moon, _____ And I was the

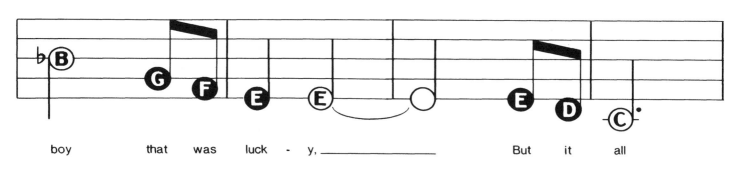

boy that was luck - y, _____ But it all

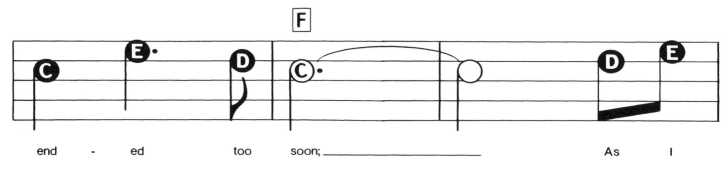

end - ed too soon; _____ As I

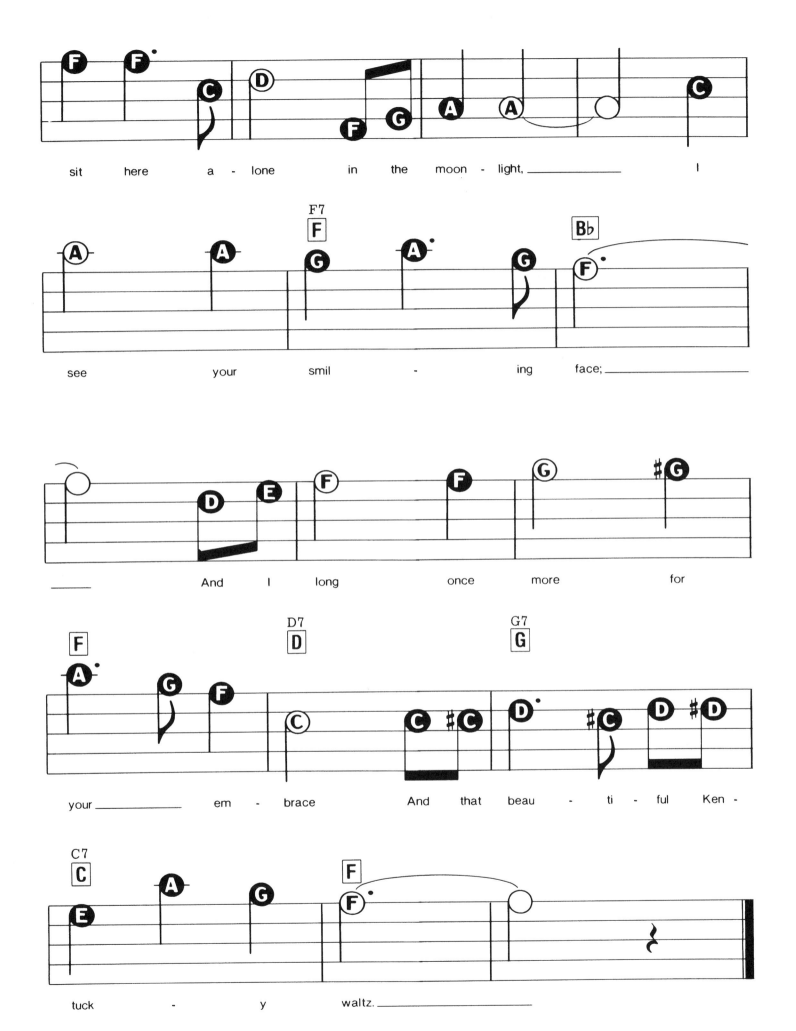

Let Me Call You Sweetheart

Registration 3
Rhythm: Waltz

Words by Beth Slater Whitson
Music by Leo Friedman

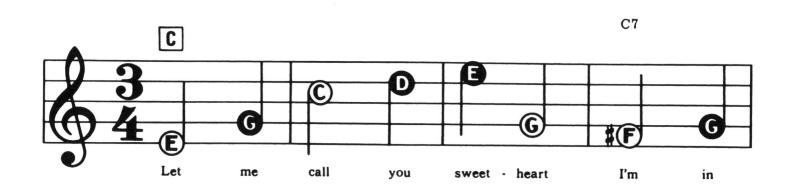

Let me call you sweet - heart I'm in

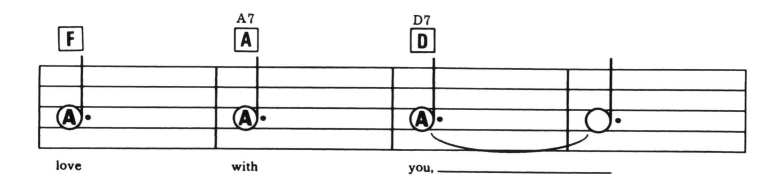

love with you, _____

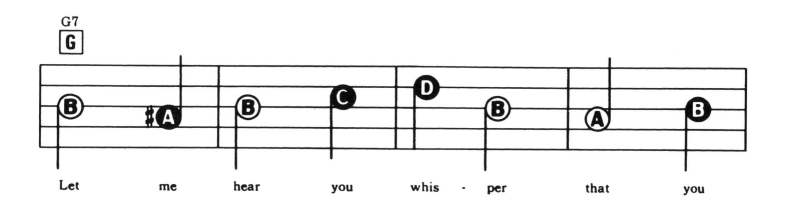

Let me hear you whis - per that you

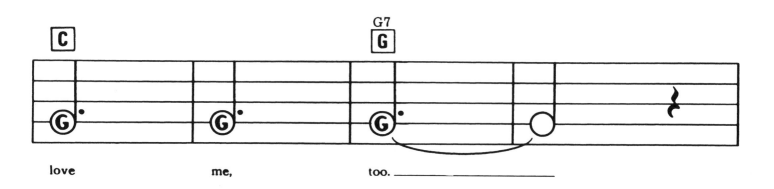

love me, too. _____

45

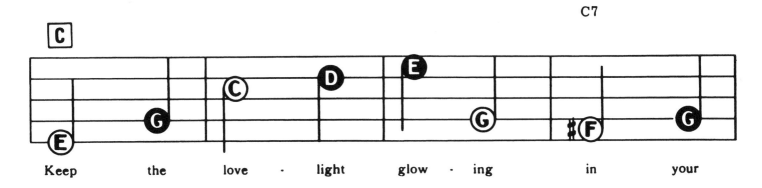

Keep   the   love - light   glow - ing   in   your

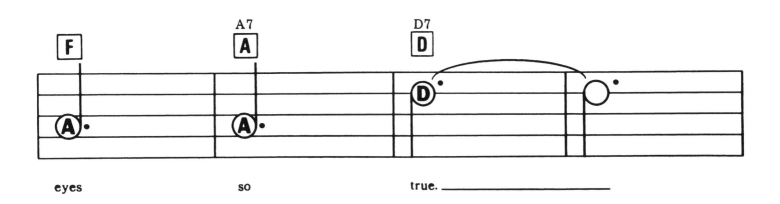

eyes   so   true. _____

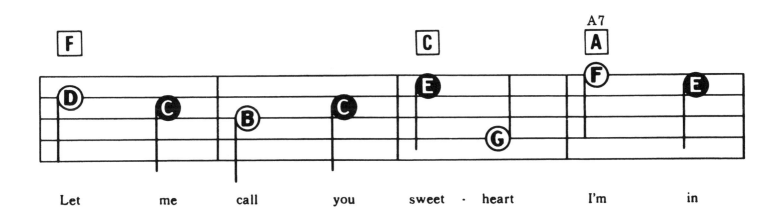

Let   me   call   you   sweet - heart   I'm   in

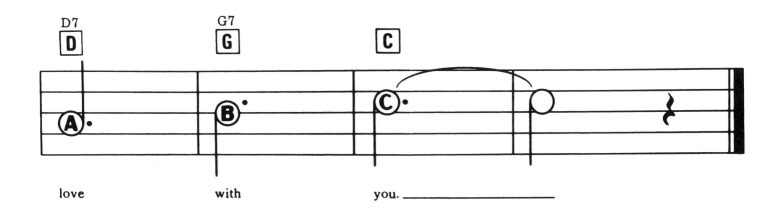

love   with   you. _____

Meet Me Tonight in Dreamland

Registration 5
Rhythm: Waltz

Words by Beth Slater Whitson
Music by Leo Friedman

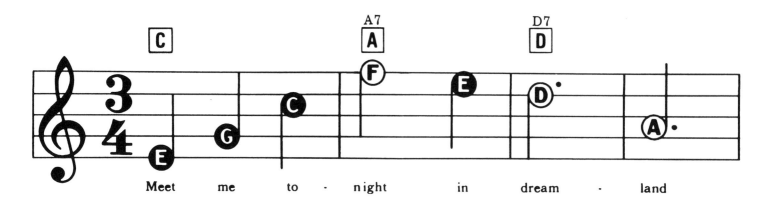

Meet me to - night in dream - land

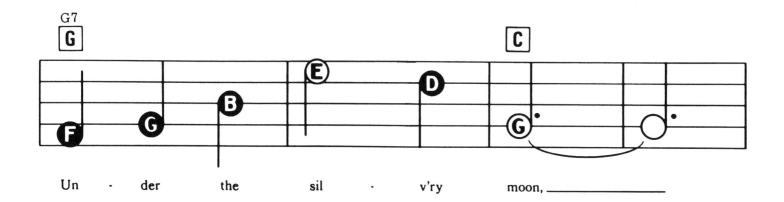

Un - der the sil - v'ry moon, _____

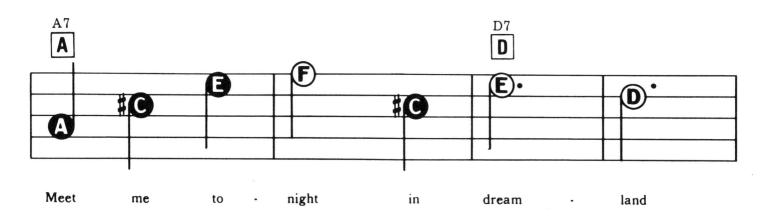

Meet me to - night in dream - land

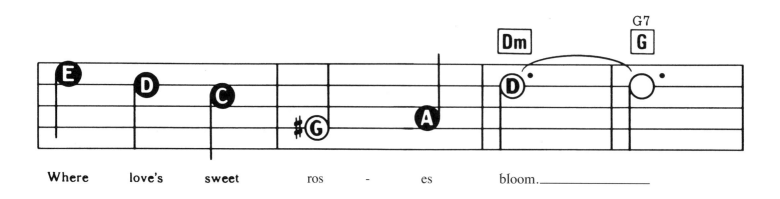

Where love's sweet ros - es bloom. _____

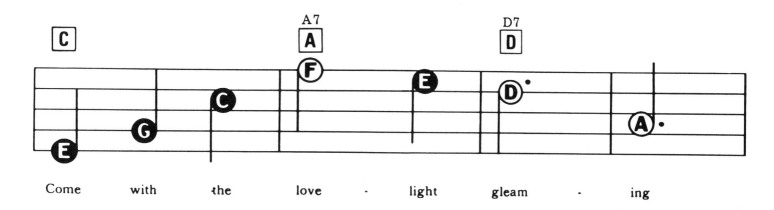

Come with the love - light gleam - ing

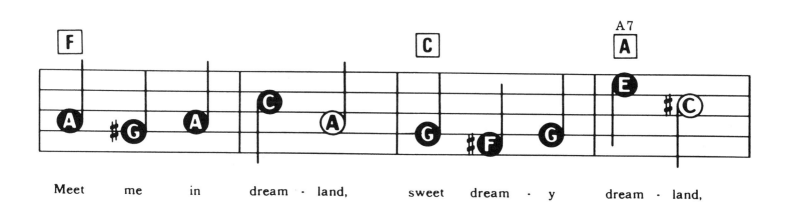

In your dear eyes of blue, _____

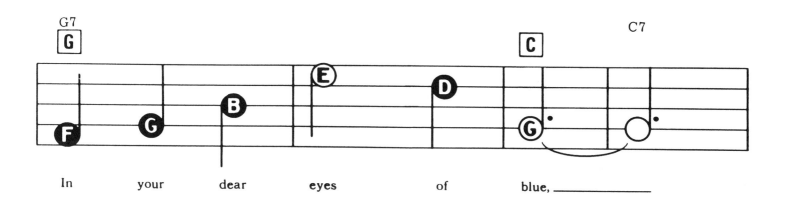

Meet me in dream - land, sweet dream - y dream - land,

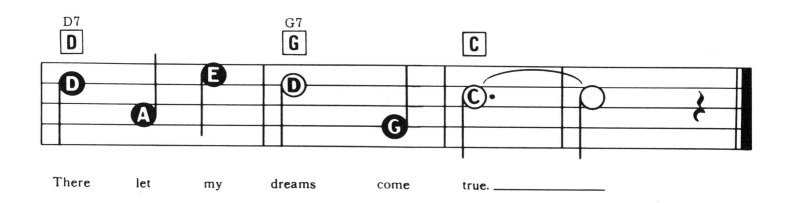

There let my dreams come true. _____

Melody of Love

Registration 10
Rhythm: Waltz

By H. Engelmann

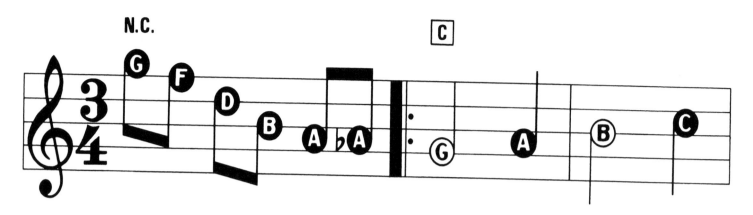

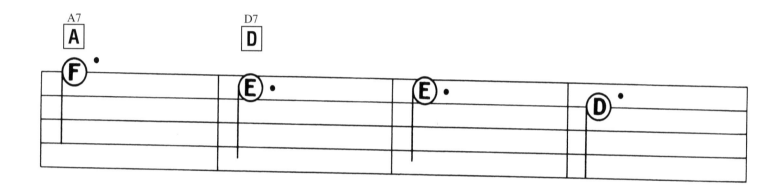

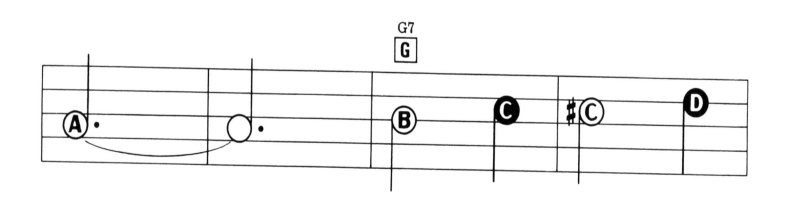

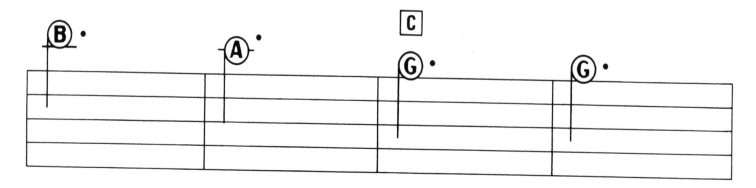

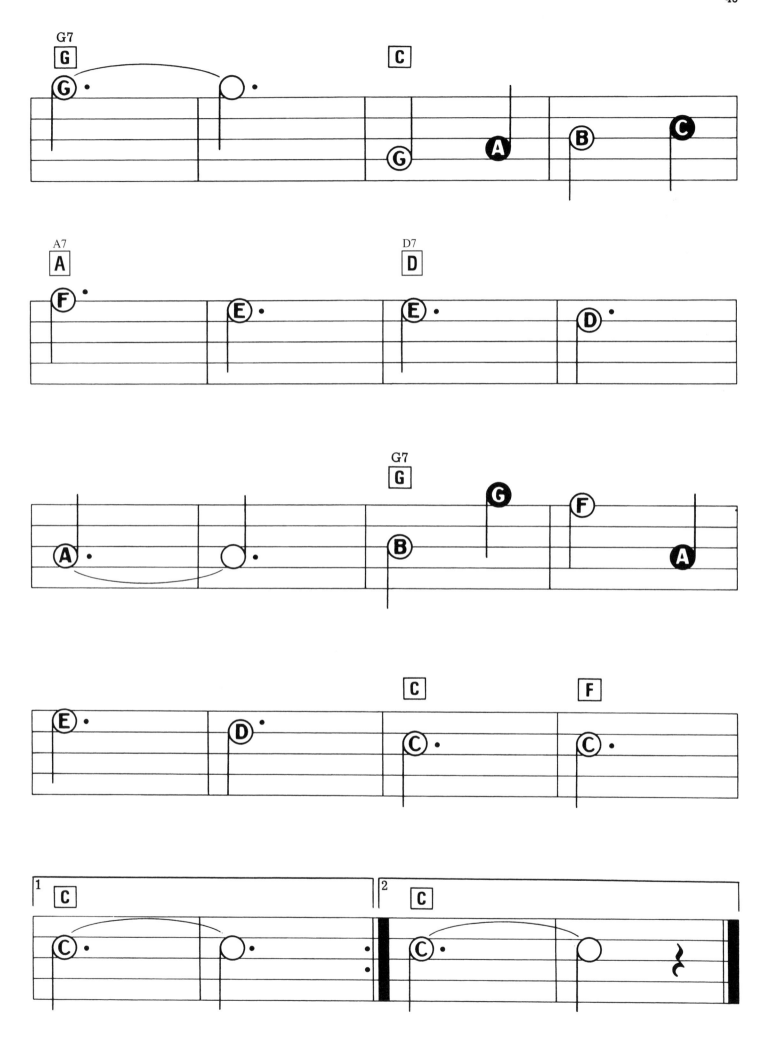

Mockin' Bird Hill

Registration 4
Rhythm: Waltz

Words and Music by
Vaughn Horton

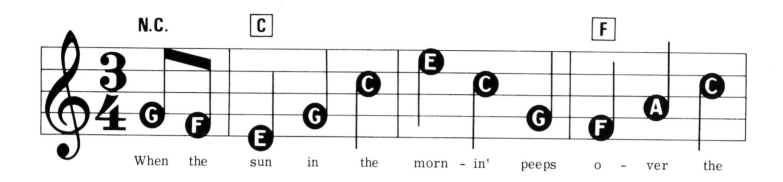

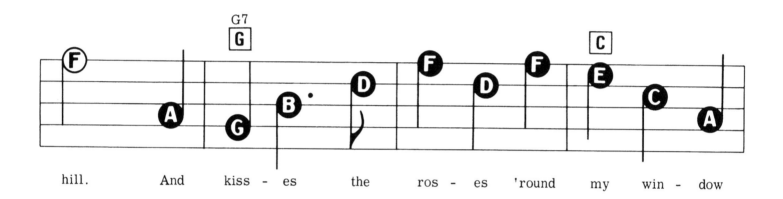

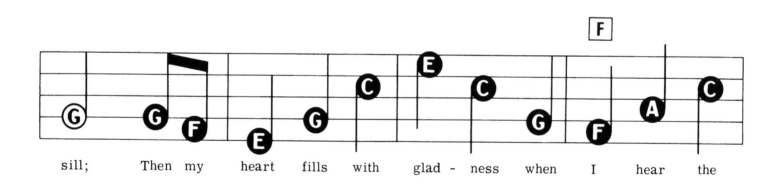

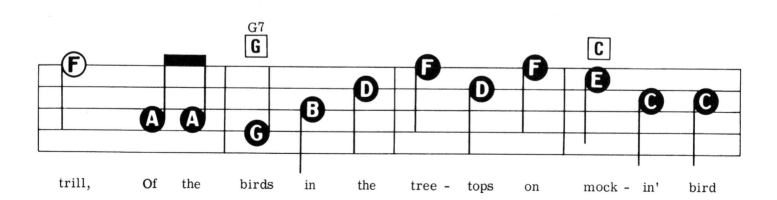

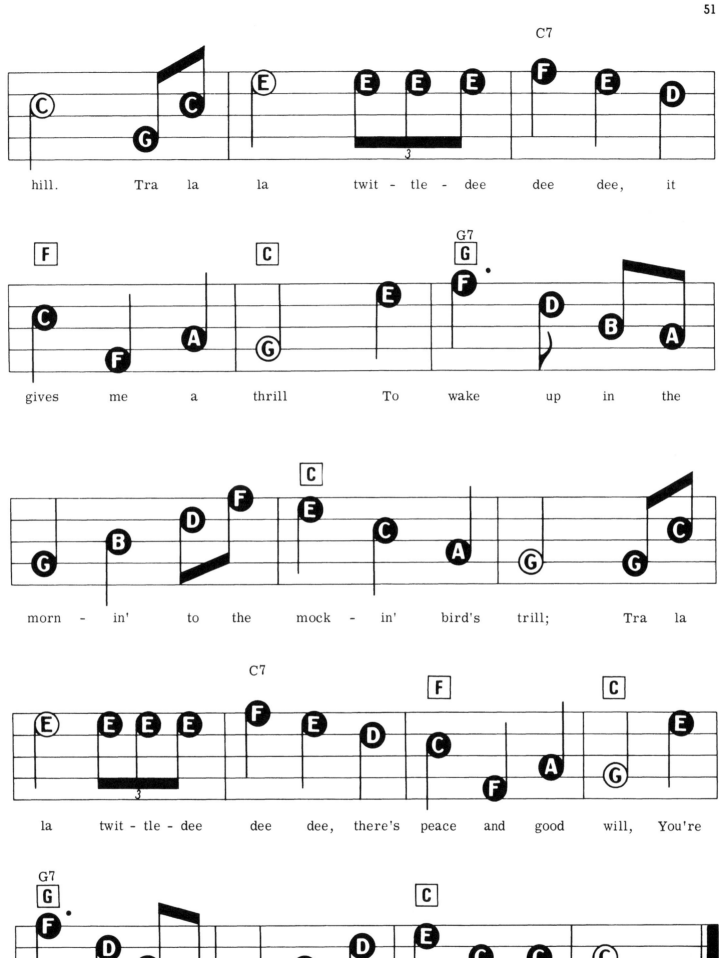

My Favorite Things
from THE SOUND OF MUSIC

Registration 1
Rhythm: Waltz

Lyrics by Oscar Hammerstein II
Music by Richard Rodgers

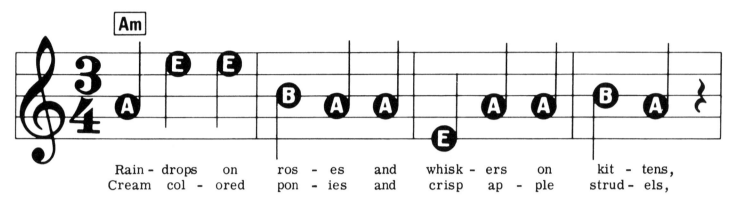

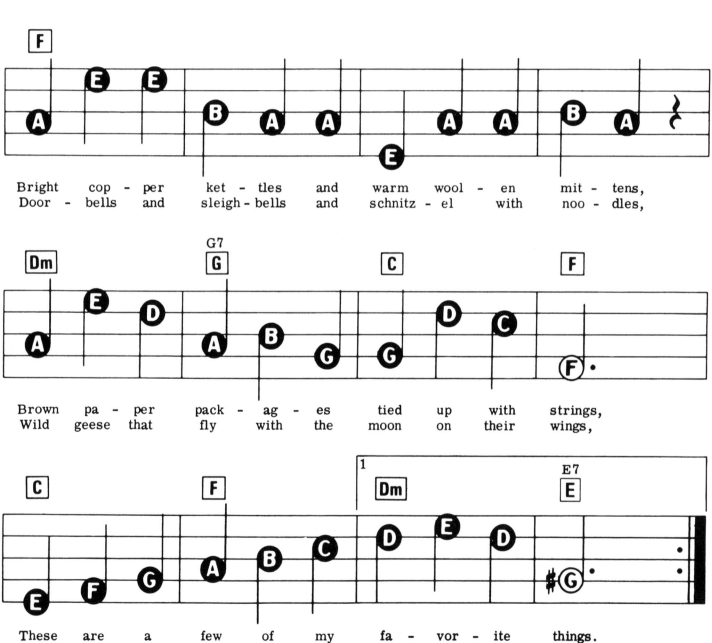

Rain - drops   on   ros - es   and   whisk - ers   on   kit - tens,
Cream col - ored   pon - ies   and   crisp   ap - ple   strud - els,

Bright   cop - per   ket - tles   and   warm   wool - en   mit - tens,
Door - bells   and   sleigh - bells   and   schnitz - el   with   noo - dles,

Brown   pa - per   pack - ag - es   tied   up   with   strings,
Wild   geese   that   fly   with   the   moon   on   their   wings,

These   are   a   few   of   my   fa - vor - ite   things.
These   are   a   few   of   my

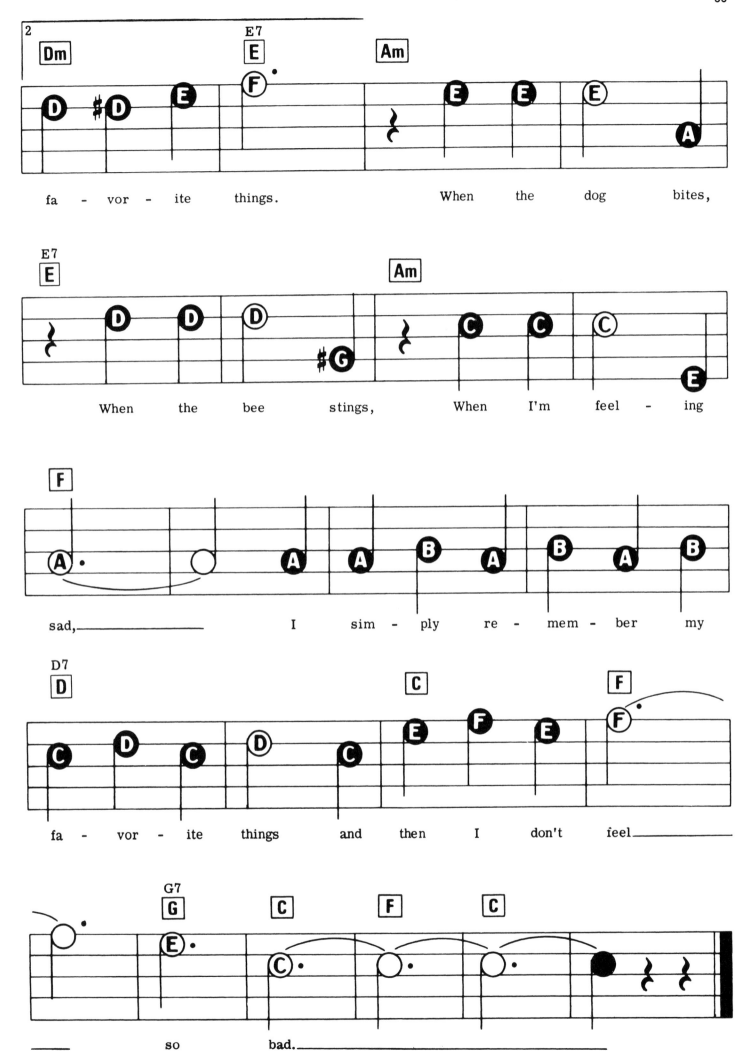

My Heart Cries for You

Registration 10
Rhythm: Waltz

Music by Percy Faith
Lyrics by Carl Sigman

If you're in Ar - i - zon - a I'll fol - low
bloom has left the ros - es since you left
un - im - por - tant quar - rel was what we

you, If you're in Min - ne - so - ta I'll be there
me, The birds have left my win - dow since you left
had, We have to learn to live with the good

too, You'll have a mil - lion chanc - es to
me, I'm lone - ly as a sail - boat that's
bad, To - geth - er we were hap - py, a -

start a - new, Be - cause my love is
lost at sea, I'm lone - ly as a
part we're sad, This lone - li - ness is

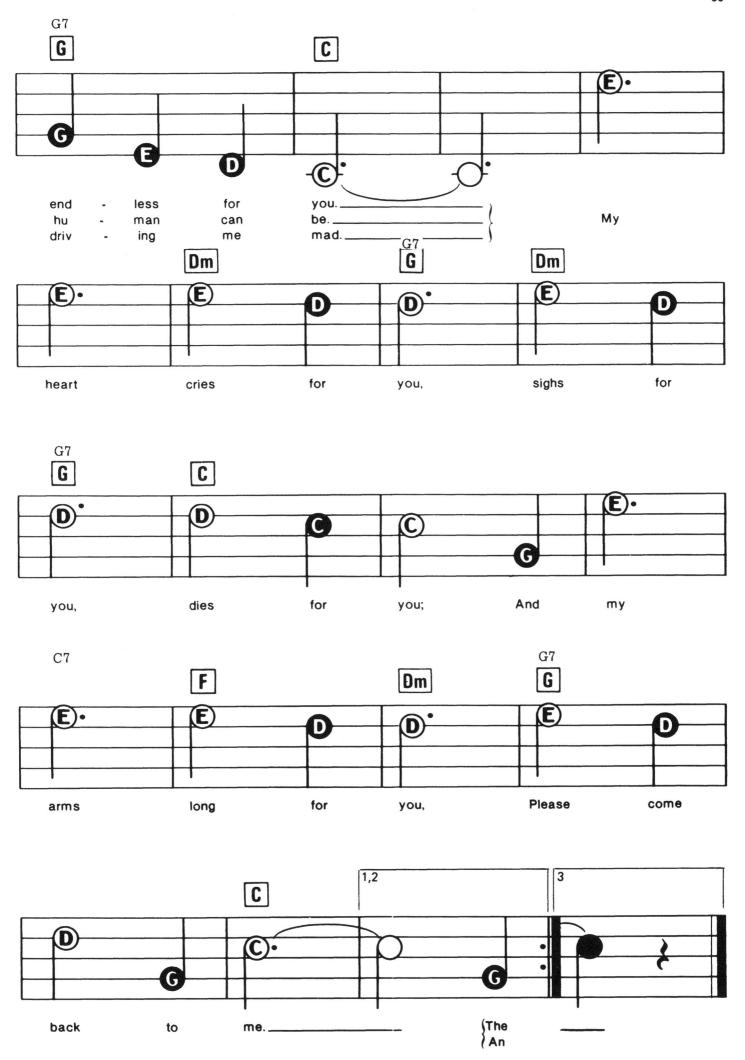

Now Is the Hour
(Maori Farewell Song)

Registration 9
Rhythm: Waltz

Words and Music by Clement Scott,
Maewa Kaithau and Dorothy Stewart

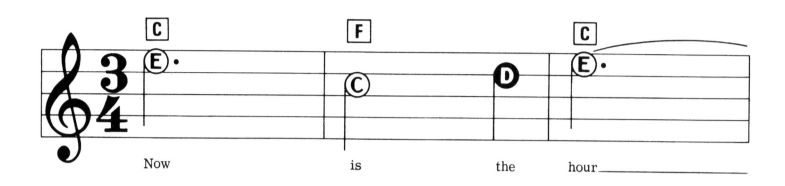

Now   is   the   hour

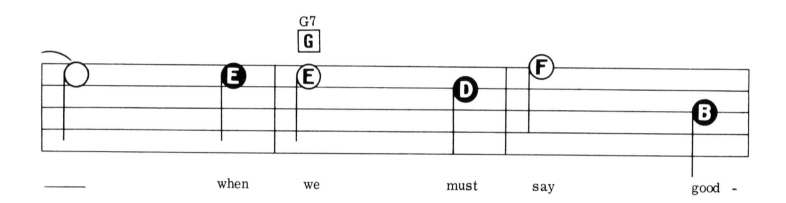

when   we   must   say   good -

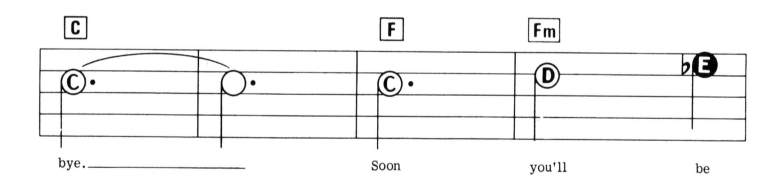

bye.   Soon   you'll   be

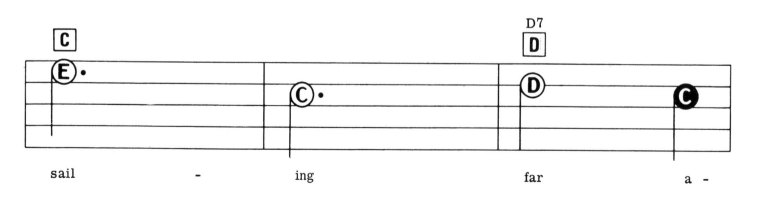

sail -   ing   far   a -

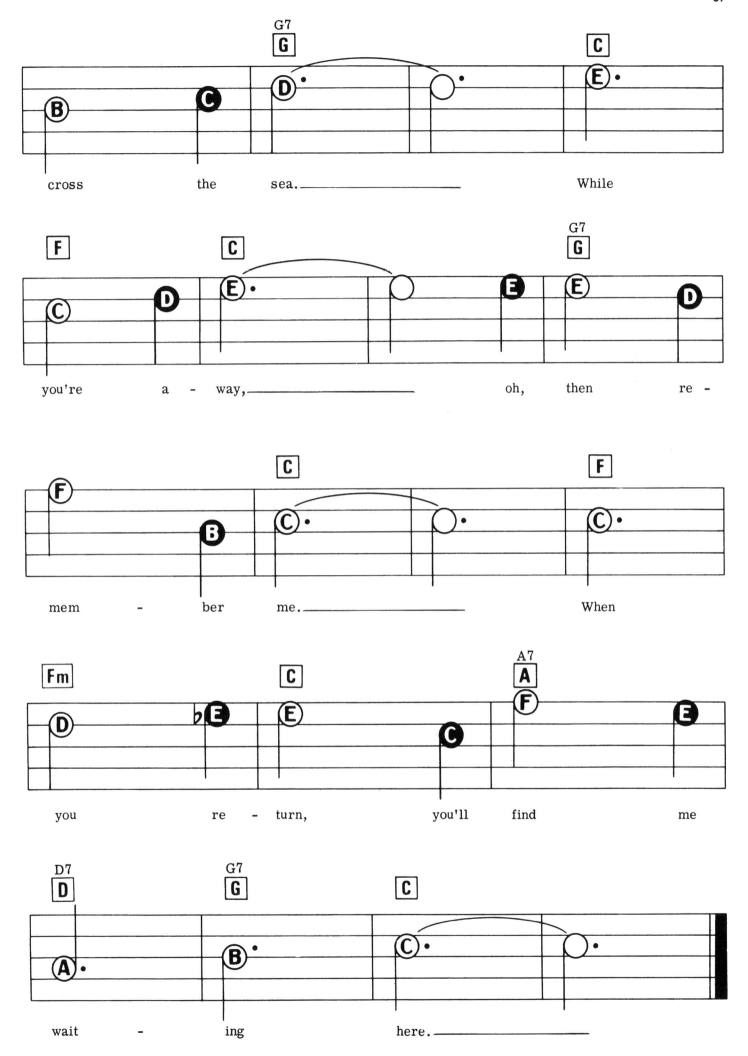

Oh, What a Beautiful Mornin'
from OKLAHOMA

Registration 5
Rhythm: Waltz

Lyrics by Oscar Hammerstein II
Music by Richard Rodgers

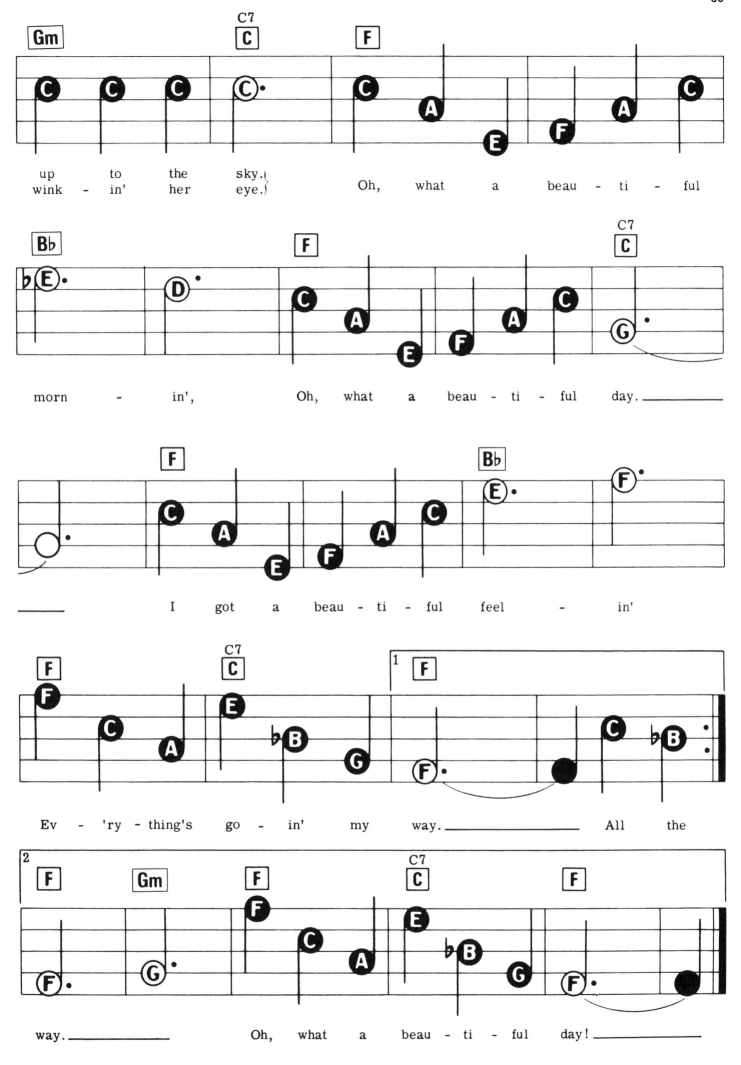

The Petite Waltz

Registration 5
Rhythm: Waltz

English Lyric by E.A. Ellington and Phyllis Claire
Music by Joe Heyne

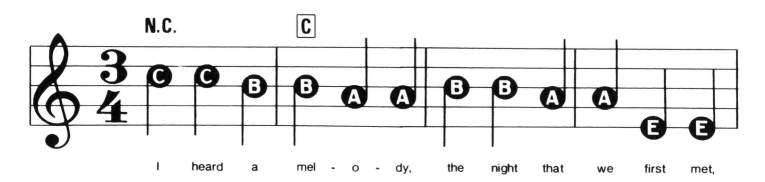

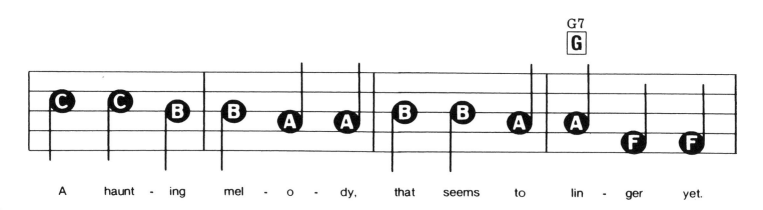

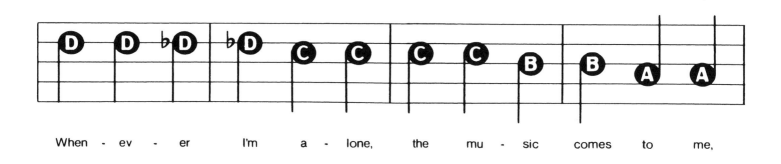

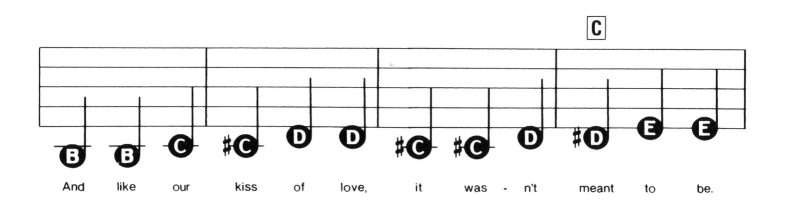

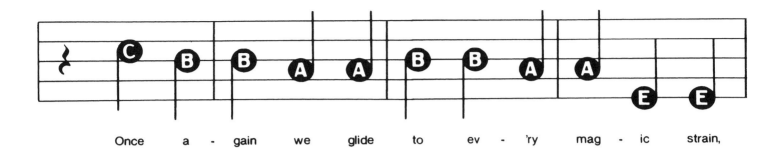

Once a - gain we glide to ev - 'ry mag - ic strain,

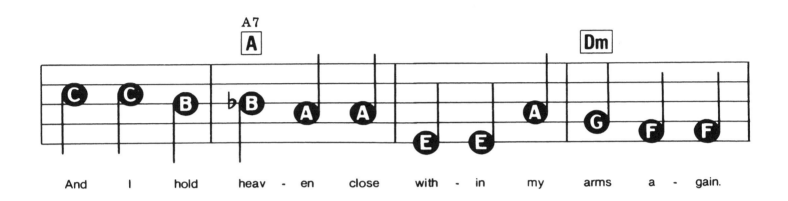

And I hold heav - en close with - in my arms a - gain.

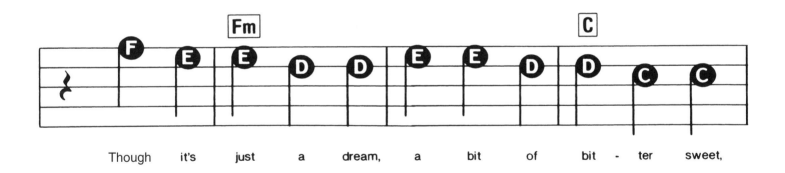

Though it's just a dream, a bit of bit - ter sweet,

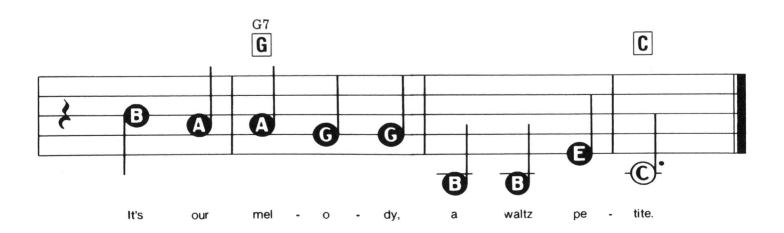

It's our mel - o - dy, a waltz pe - tite.

Pigalle

Registration 5
Rhythm: Waltz

English Lyric by Charles Newman
French Lyric by Geo Koger, Georges Ulmer and Guy Luypaerts
Music by Georges Ulmer and Guy Luypaerts

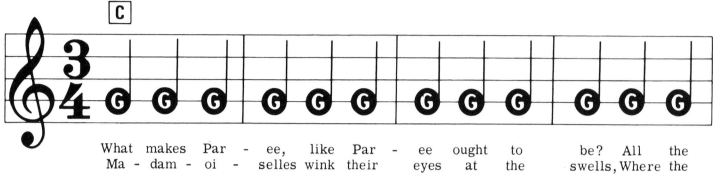

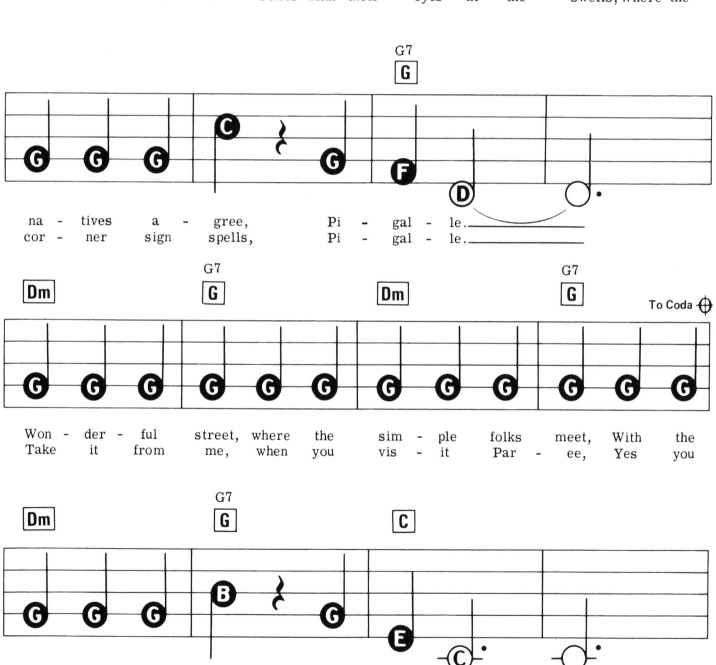

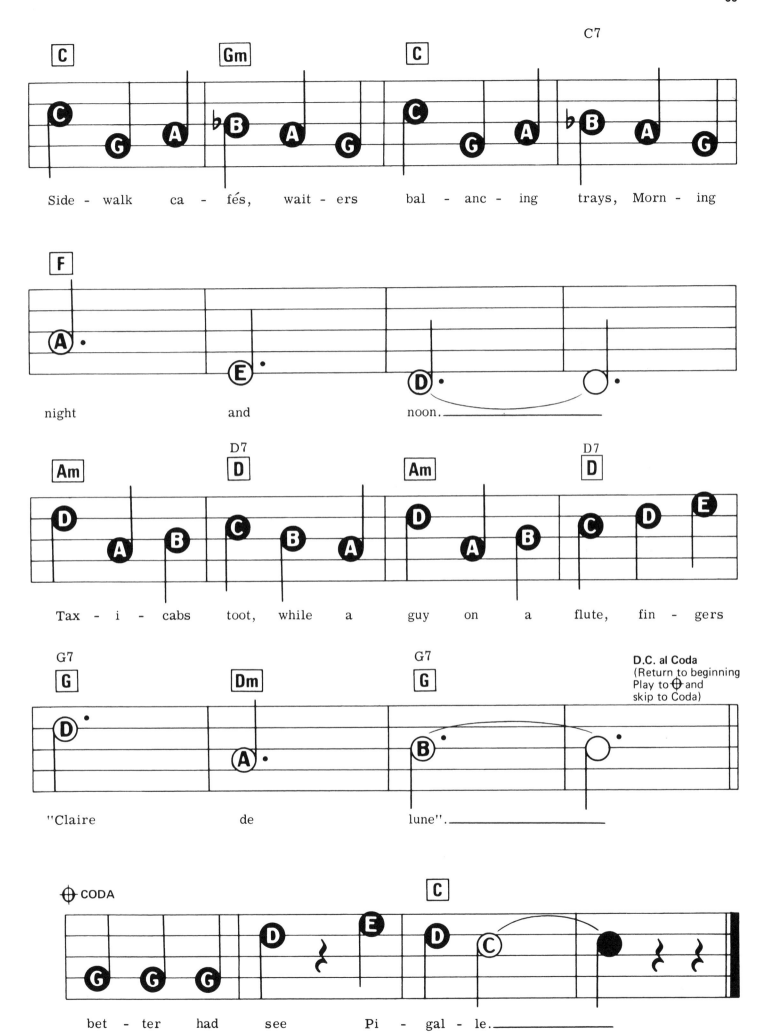

Sidewalks of New York

Registration 10
Rhythm: Waltz

Words and Music by Charles B. Lawlor
and James W. Blake

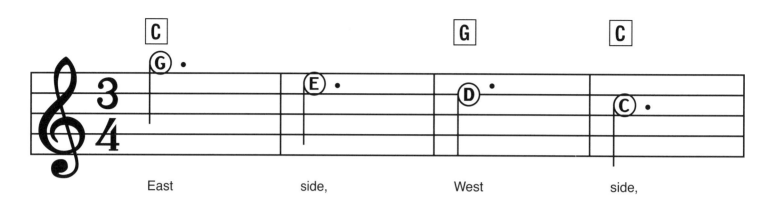

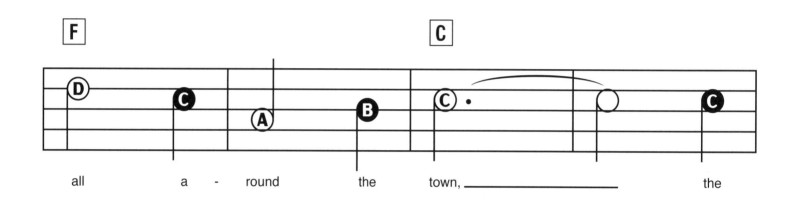

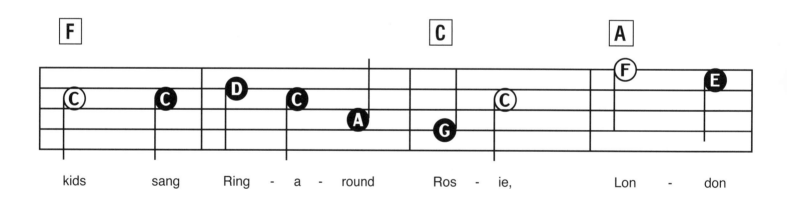

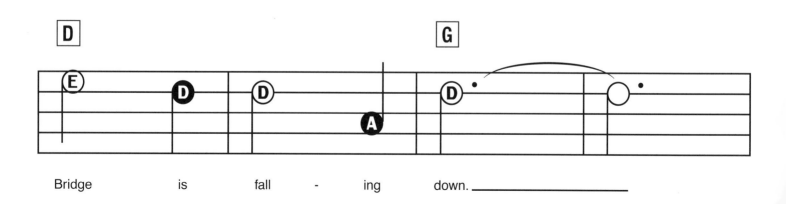

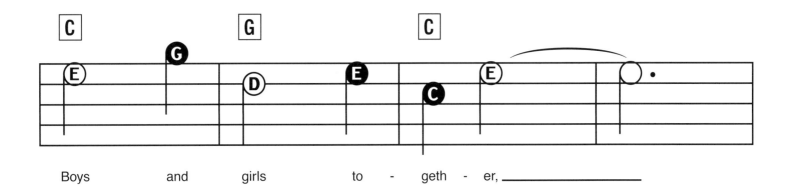

Boys and girls to - geth - er, _____

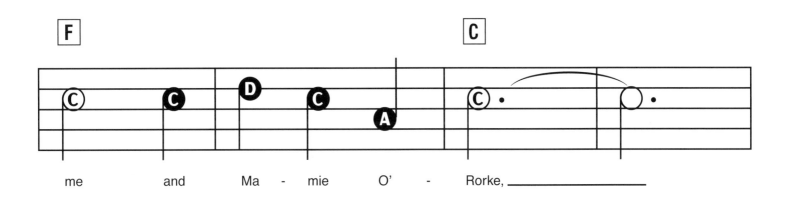

me and Ma - mie O' - Rorke, _____

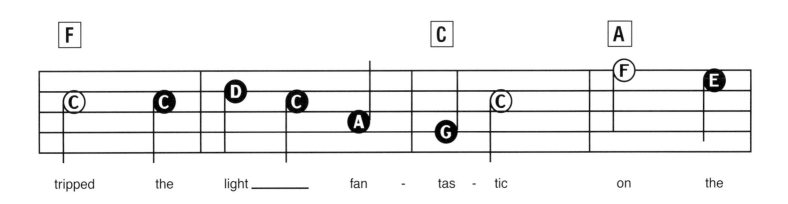

tripped the light _____ fan - tas - tic on the

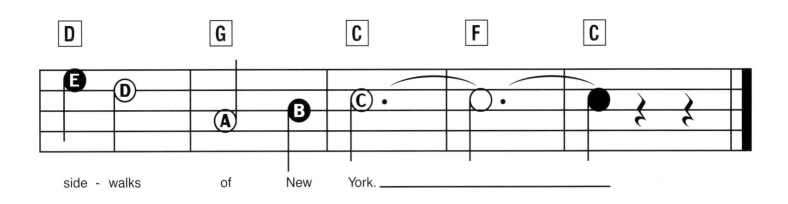

side - walks of New York. _____

The Sweetheart of Sigma Chi

Registration 1
Rhythm: Waltz

Words by Byron D. Stokes
Music by F. Dudleigh Vernor

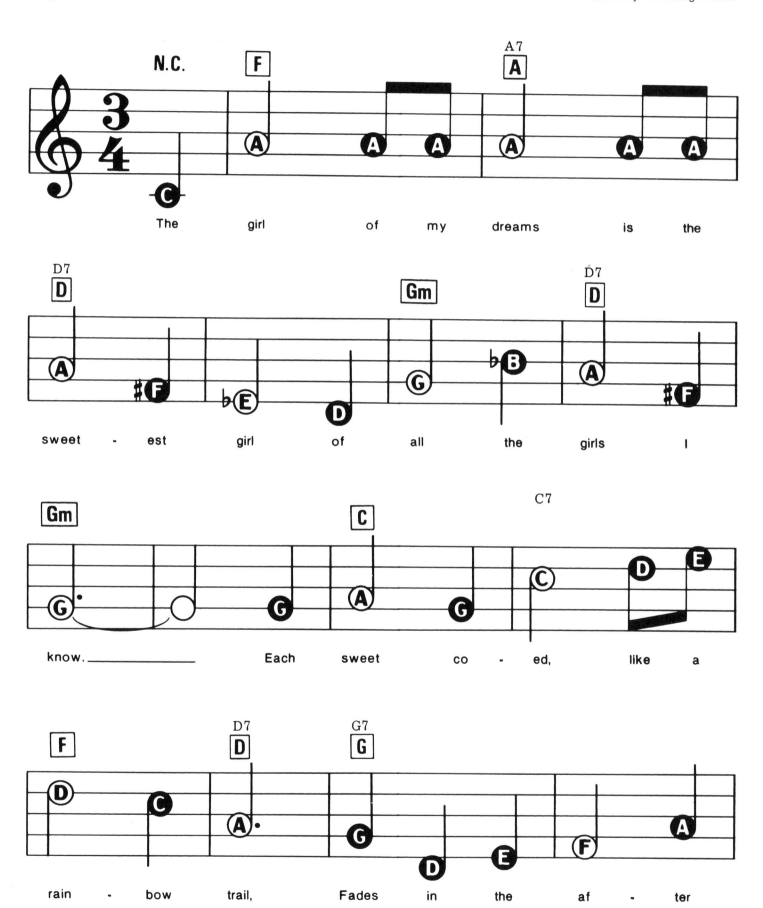

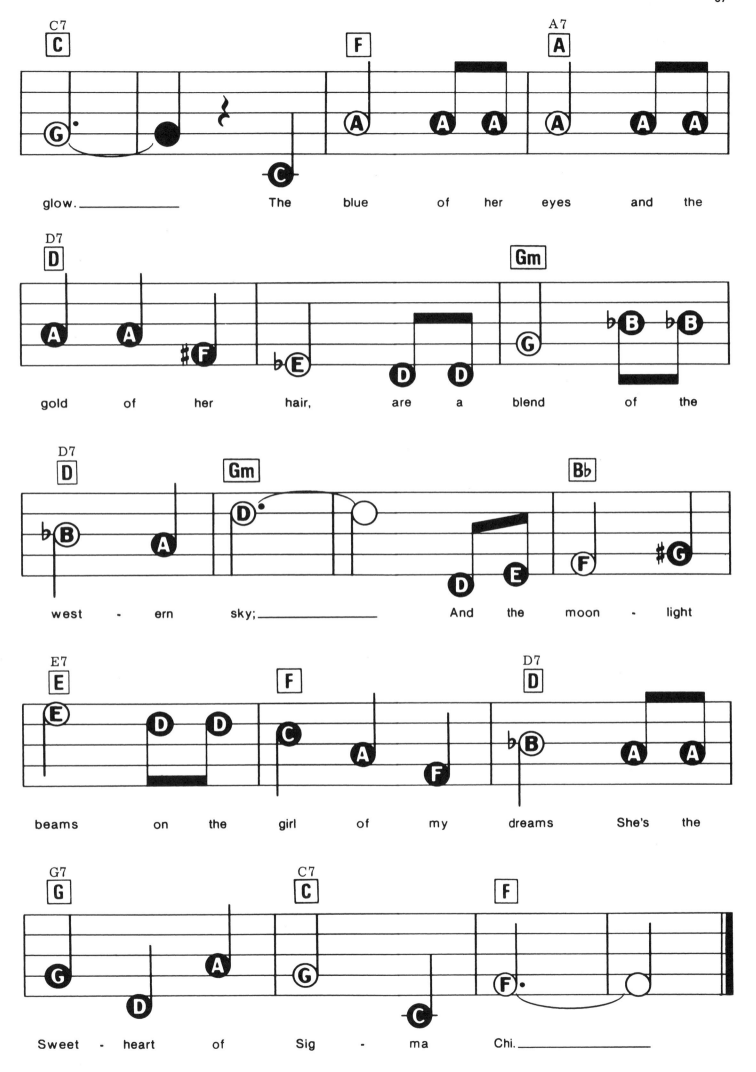

Tennessee Waltz

Registration 4
Rhythm: Waltz

Words and Music by Redd Stewart
and Pee Wee King

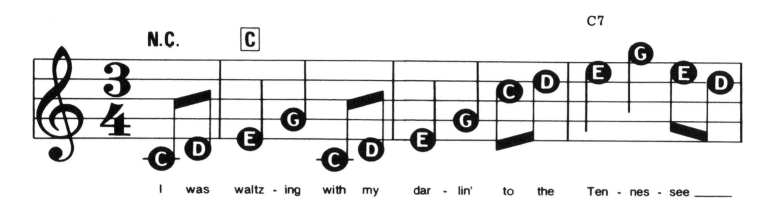

I was waltz - ing with my dar - lin' to the Ten - nes - see _____

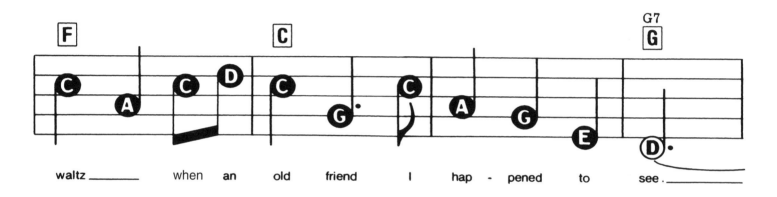

waltz _____ when an old friend I hap - pened to see. _____

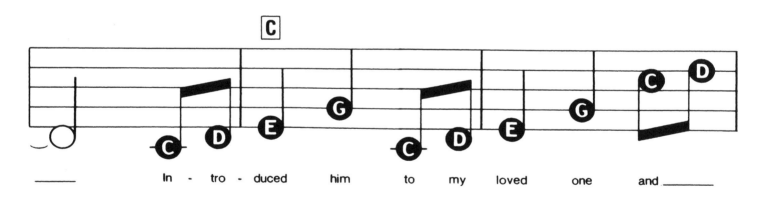

_____ In - tro - duced him to my loved one and _____

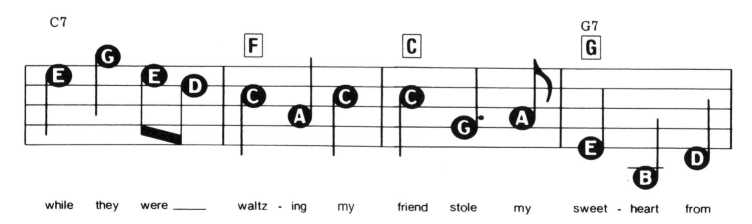

while they were _____ waltz - ing my friend stole my sweet - heart from

69

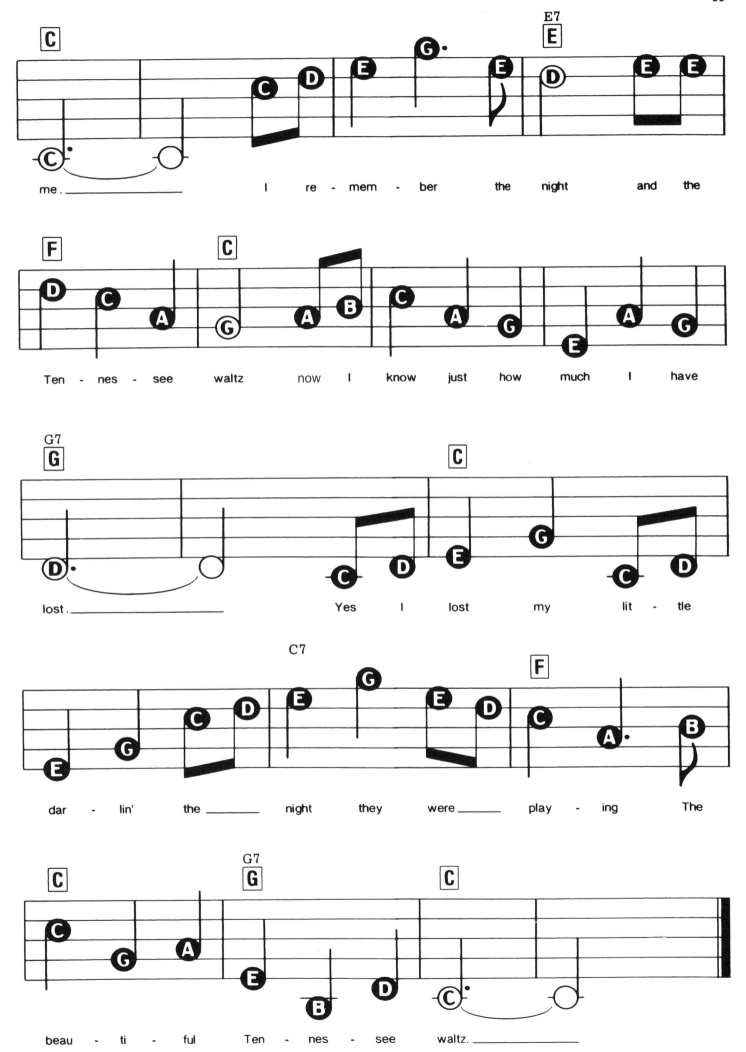

True Love
from HIGH SOCIETY

Registration 4
Rhythm: Waltz

Words and Music by
Cole Porter

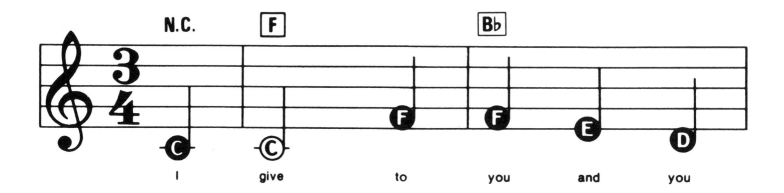

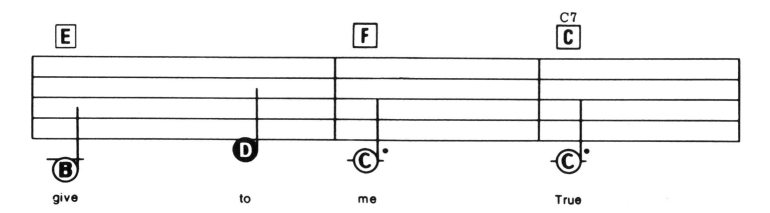

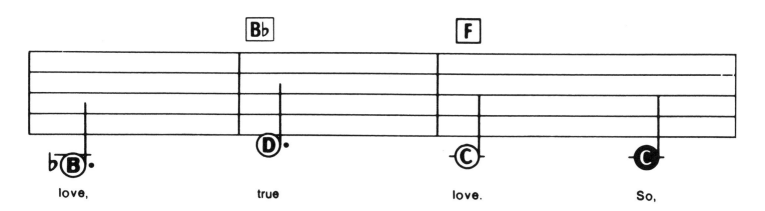

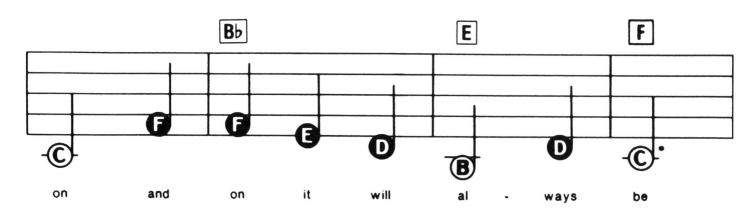

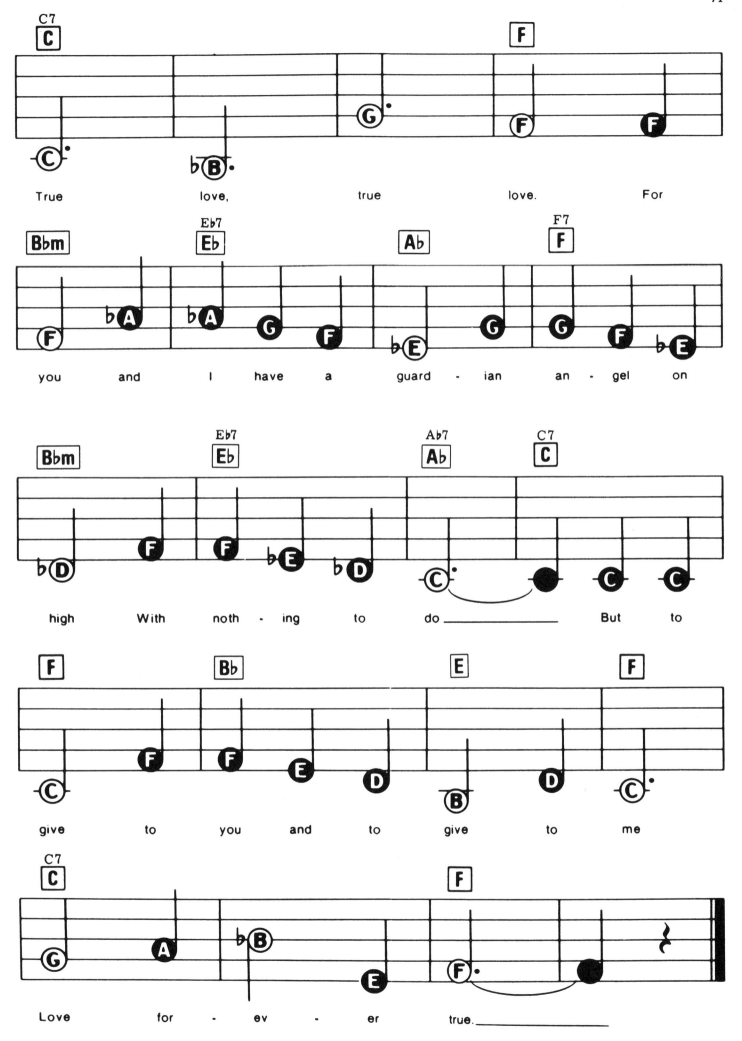

Under Paris Skies

Registration 10
Rhythm: Waltz

English Words by Kim Gannon
French Words by Jean Drejac
Music by Hubert Giraud

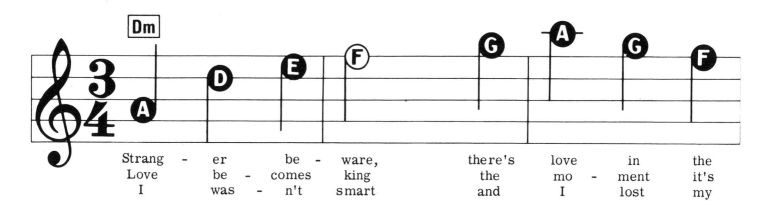

Strang - er be - ware, there's love in the
Love be - comes king the mo - ment it's
I was - n't smart and I lost my

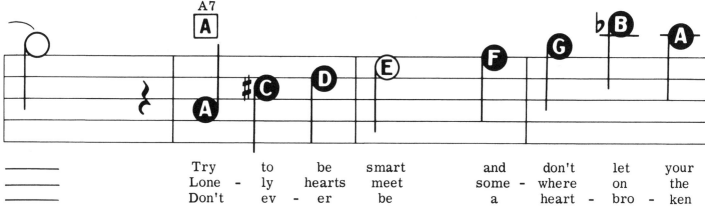

air, un - der Par - is skies.
spring, un - der Par - is skies.
heart, un - der Par - is skies.

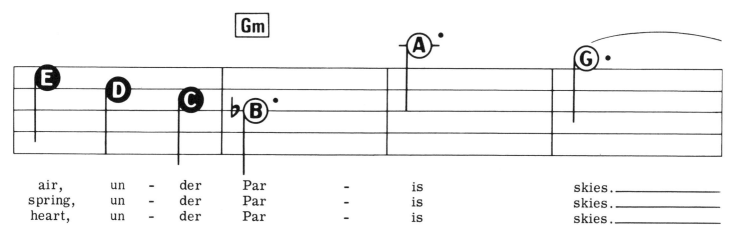

Try to be smart and don't let your
Lone - ly hearts meet some - where on the
Don't ev - er be a heart - bro - ken

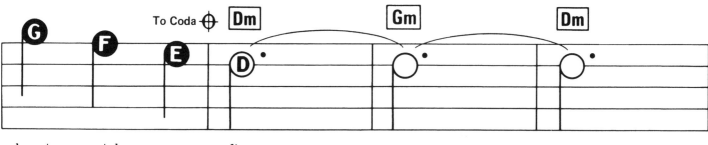

heart catch on fire.
street of de - sire.
strang - er like

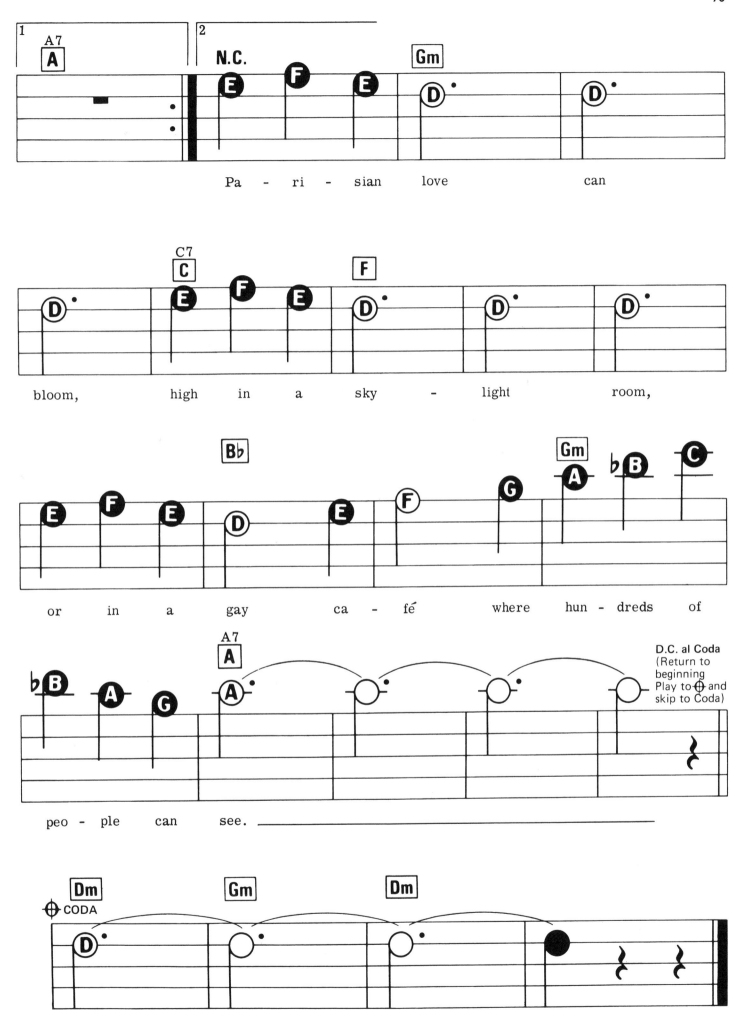

When Irish Eyes Are Smiling

Registration 3
Rhythm: Waltz

Words by Chauncey Olcott and George Graff, Jr.
Music by Ernest R. Ball

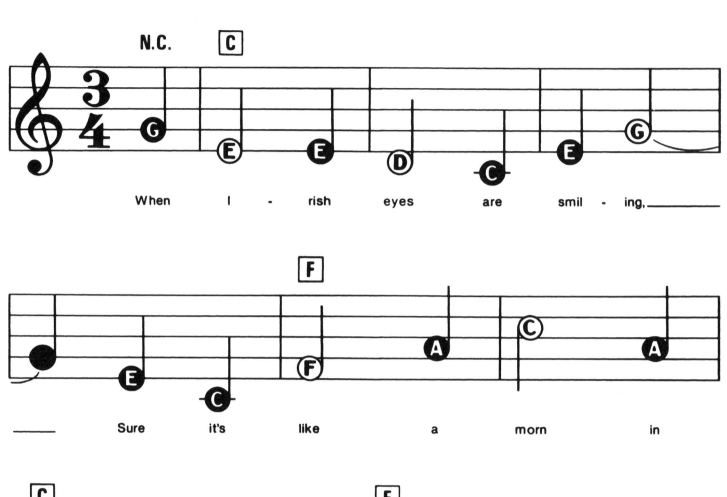

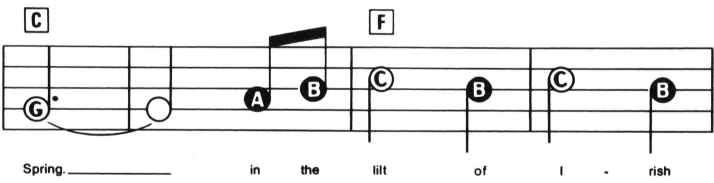

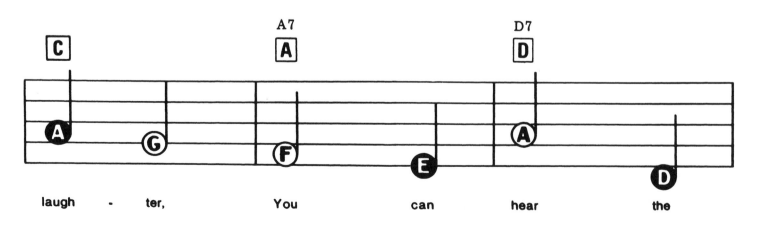

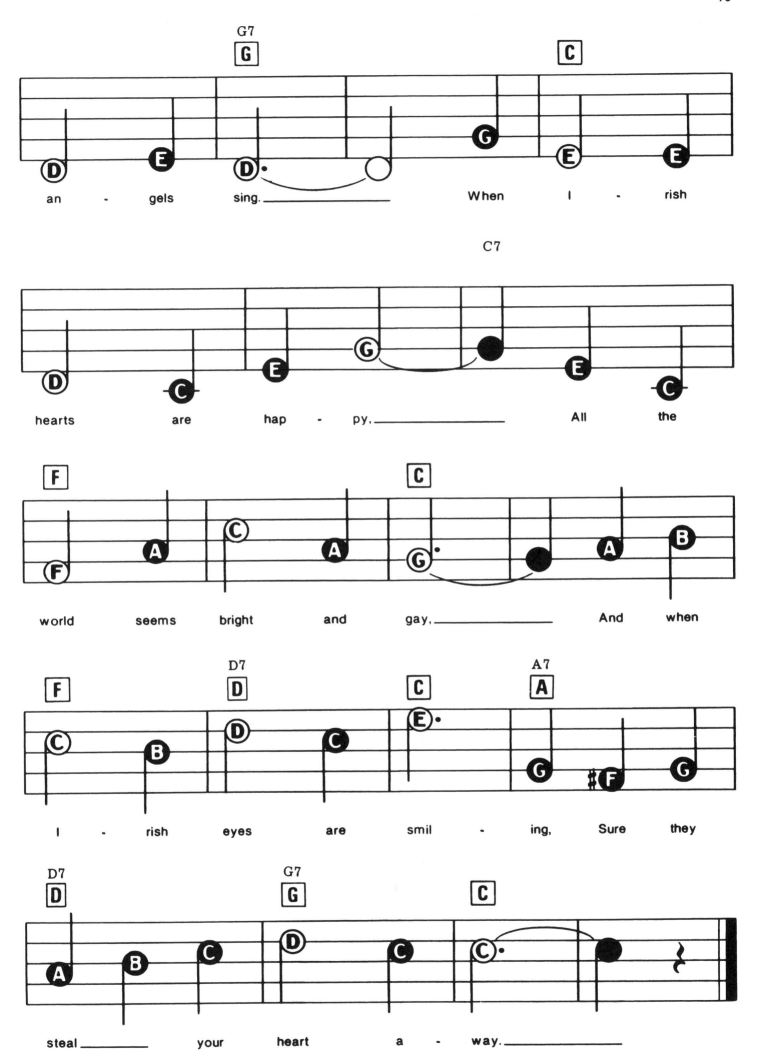

Where the Blue of the Night
(Meets the Gold of the Day)

Registration 1
Rhythm: Waltz

Lyric and Music by Fred E. Ahlert,
Bing Crosby and Roy Turk

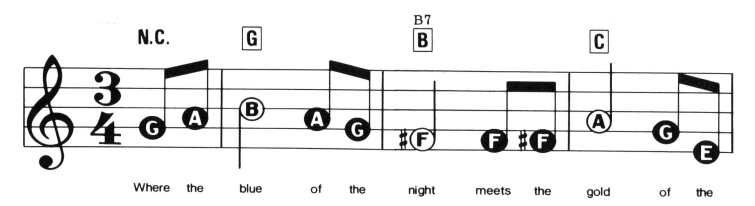

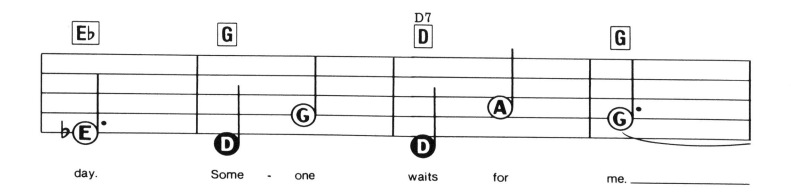

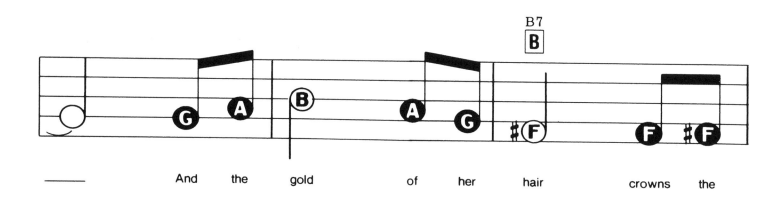

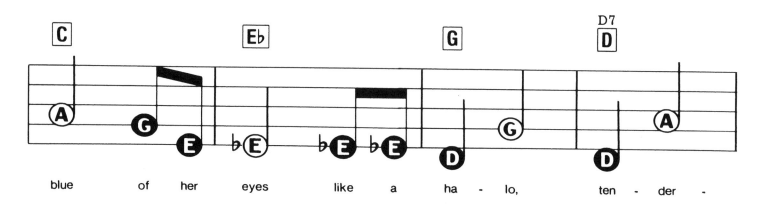

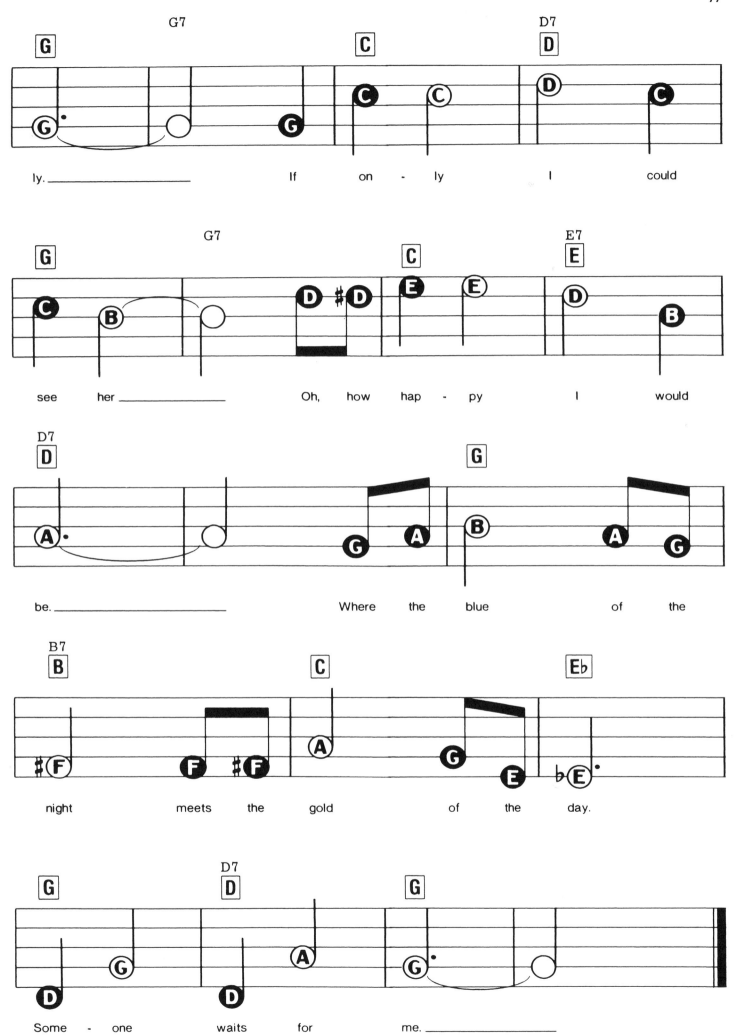

The Wonderful World of the Young

Registration 3
Rhythm: Waltz

Words and Music by
Sid Tepper and Roy C. Bennett

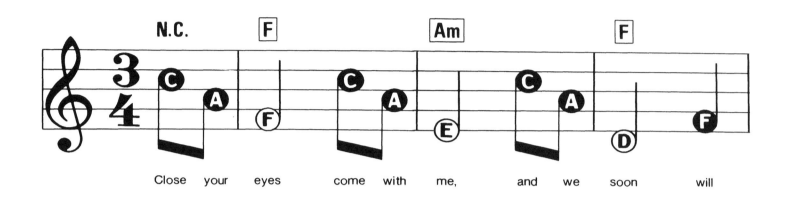

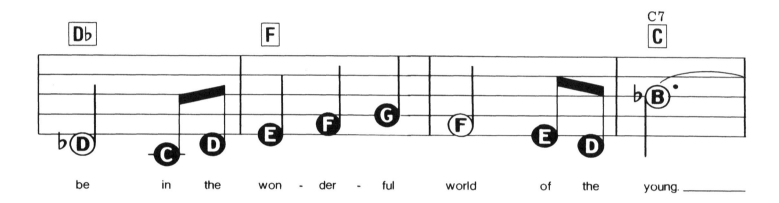

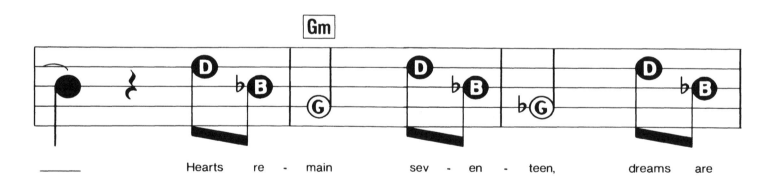

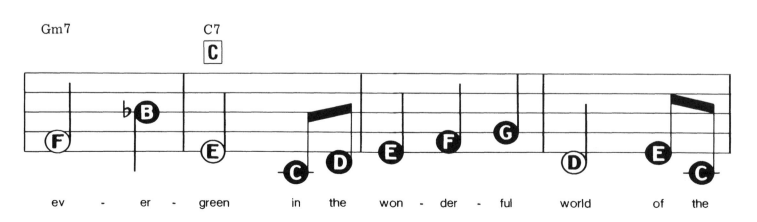

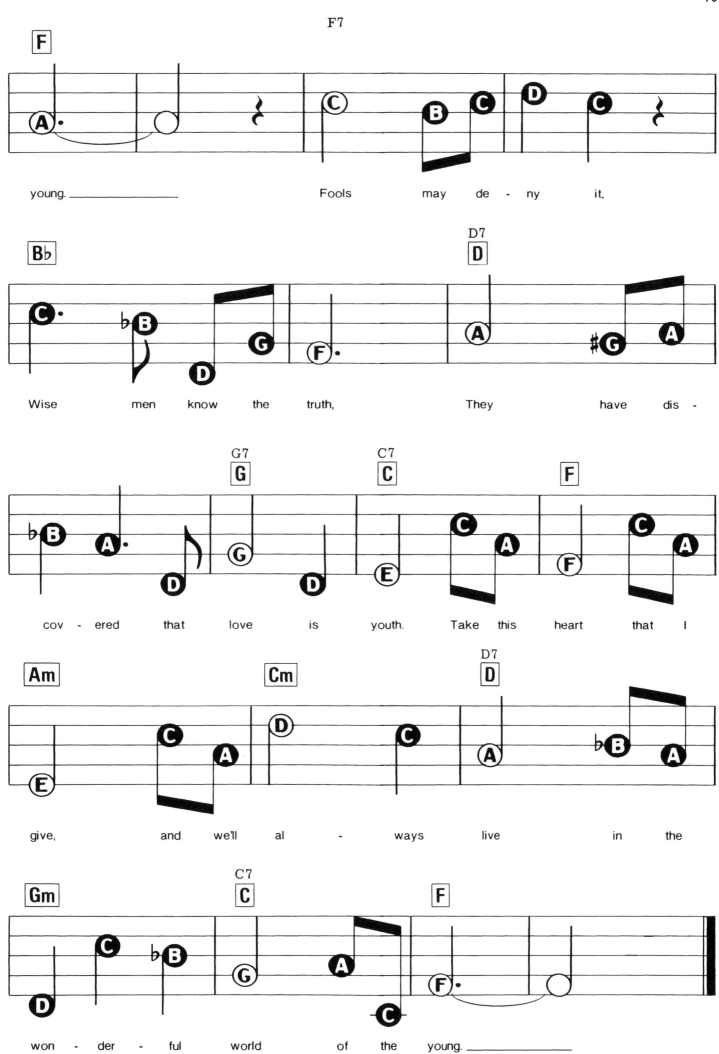

Wunderbar
from KISS ME, KATE

Registration 4
Rhythm: Waltz

Words and Music by
Cole Porter

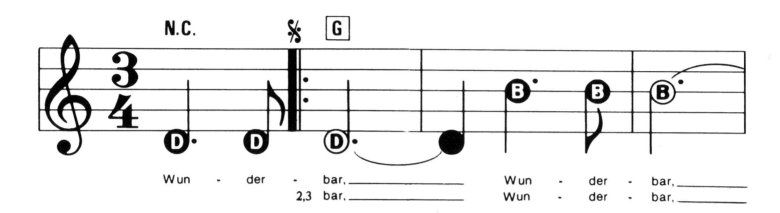

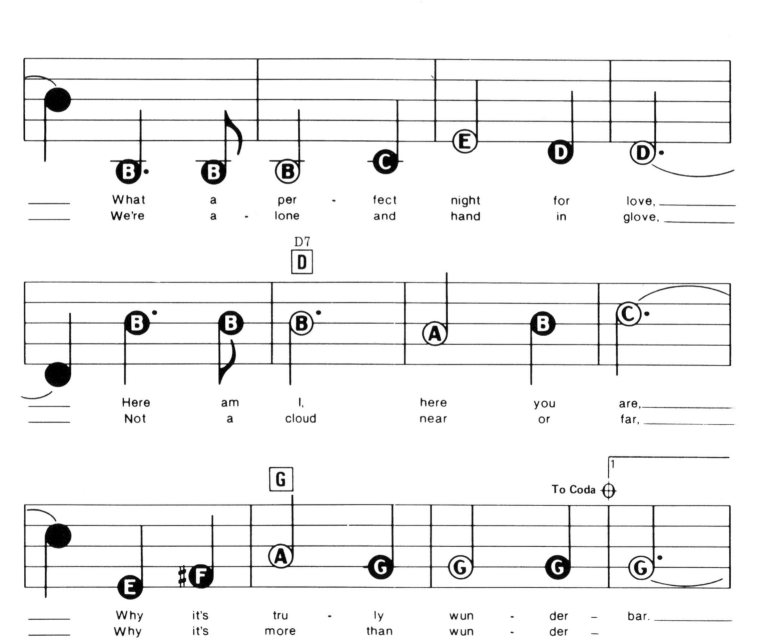

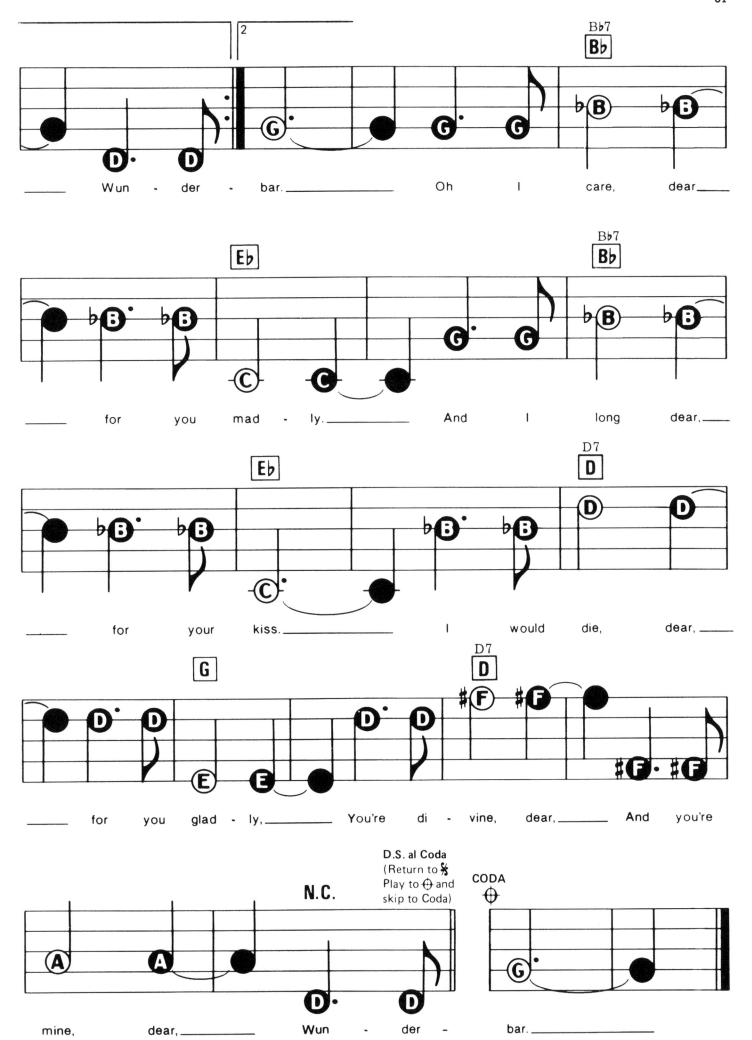

You Can't Be True Dear
(Du kannst nicht treu sein)

Registration 2
Rhythm: Waltz

English Lyric by Hal Cotton
Original German Text by Gerhard Ebeler
Music by Hans Otten and Ken Griffin

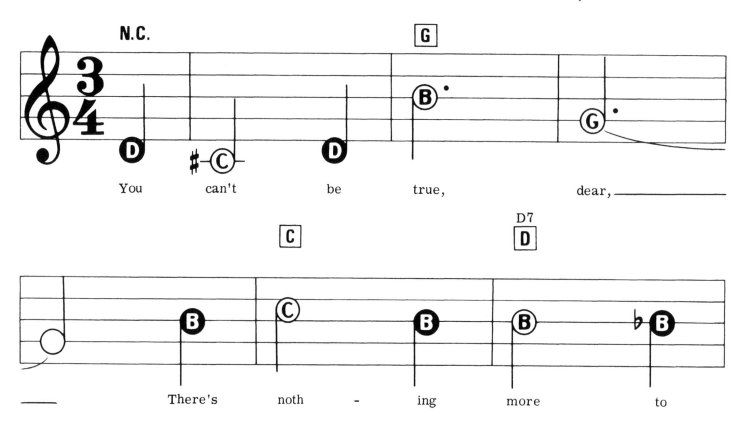

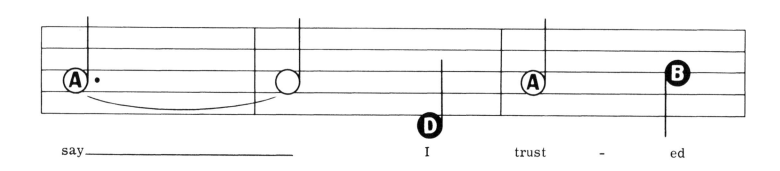

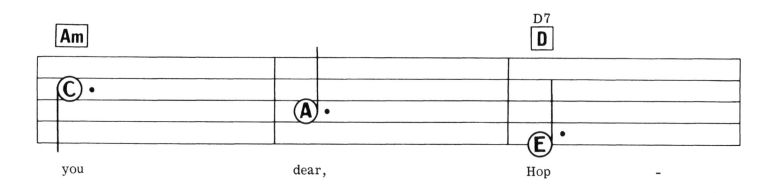

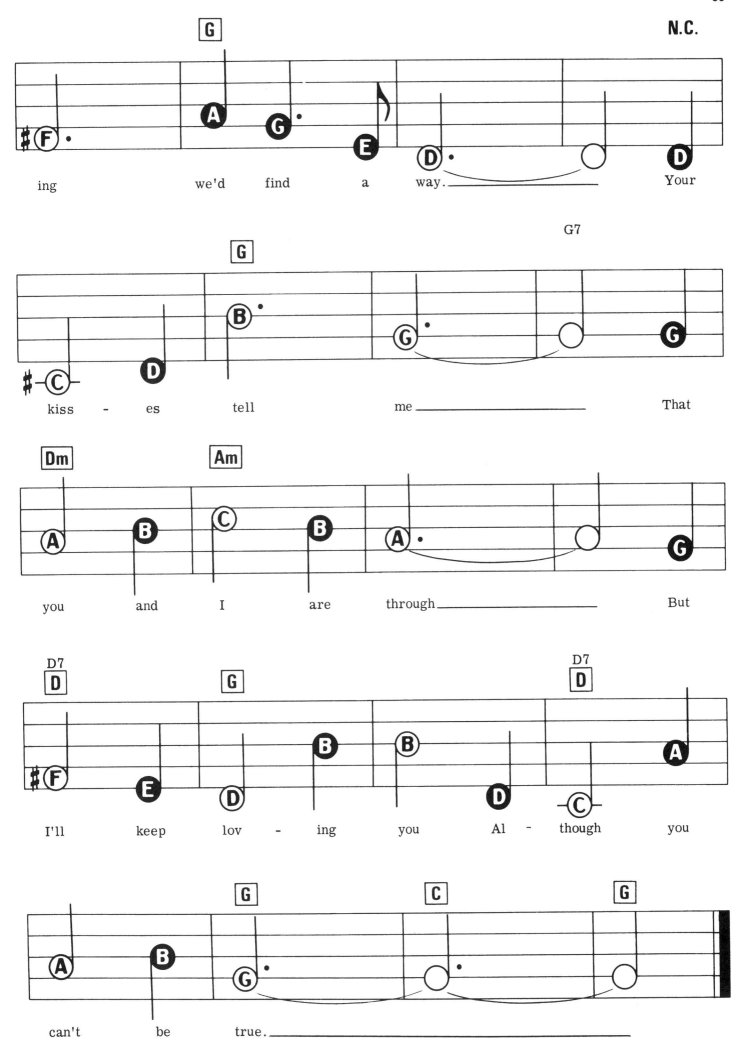

Registration Guide

- Match the Registration number on the song to the corresponding numbered category below. Select and activate an instrumental sound available on your instrument.

- Choose an automatic rhythm appropriate to the mood and style of the song. (Consult your Owner's Guide for proper operation of automatic rhythm features.)

- Adjust the tempo and volume controls to comfortable settings.

Registration

1	Mellow	Flutes, Clarinet, Oboe, Flugel Horn, Trombone, French Horn, Organ Flutes
2	Ensemble	Brass Section, Sax Section, Wind Ensemble, Full Organ, Theater Organ
3	Strings	Violin, Viola, Cello, Fiddle, String Ensemble, Pizzicato, Organ Strings
4	Guitars	Acoustic/Electric Guitars, Banjo, Mandolin, Dulcimer, Ukulele, Hawaiian Guitar
5	Mallets	Vibraphone, Marimba, Xylophone, Steel Drums, Bells, Celesta, Chimes
6	Liturgical	Pipe Organ, Hand Bells, Vocal Ensemble, Choir, Organ Flutes
7	Bright	Saxophones, Trumpet, Mute Trumpet, Synth Leads, Jazz/Gospel Organs
8	Piano	Piano, Electric Piano, Honky Tonk Piano, Harpsichord, Clavi
9	Novelty	Melodic Percussion, Wah Trumpet, Synth, Whistle, Kazoo, Perc. Organ
10	Bellows	Accordion, French Accordion, Mussette, Harmonica, Pump Organ, Bagpipes

Each book in this exciting new series comes with a CD of complete professional performances, and includes matching custom arrangements in our famous E-Z Play® Today format. With these books you can:

• Listen to complete professional performances of each of the songs

• Play the arrangements along with the recorded performances

• Sing along with the full performances; and/or play the arrangements as solos, without the disk.

SONG FAVORITES WITH 3 CHORDS • VOLUME 1
15 songs, including: Can Can Polka • For He's a Jolly Good Fellow • Kum Ba Yah • Oh! Susanna • On Top of Old Smoky • Ta-Ra-Ra-Boom-De-Ay • When the Saints Go Marching In • Yankee Doodle • and more. **00100180**

CHILDREN'S SONGS • VOLUME 2
16 songs, including: Alphabet Song • Chopsticks • Frere Jacques (Are You Sleeping?) • I've Been Working on the Railroad • Jack and Jill • Looby Loo • Mary Had a Little Lamb • The Mulberry Bush • This Old Man • Three Blind Mice • and more. **00100181**

HYMN FAVORITES • VOLUME 3
15 songs, including: Abide with Me • Blessed Assurance • The Church's One Foundation • Faith of Our Fathers • The Old Rugged Cross • Onward, Christian Soldiers • Rock of Ages • Sweet By and By • Were You There? • and more. **00100182**

COUNTRY • VOLUME 4
14 songs, including: Crazy • Gentle on My Mind • Green Green Grass of Home • I Walk the Line • Jambalaya (On the Bayou) • King of the Road • Make the World Go Away • Son-Of-A-Preacher Man • Your Cheatin' Heart • and more. **00100183**

LENNON & McCARTNEY • VOLUME 7
10 songs, including: Eleanor Rigby • Hey Jude • In My Life • The Long and Winding Road • Love Me Do • Nowhere Man • Please Please Me • Sgt. Pepper's Lonely Hearts Club Band • Strawberry Fields Forever • Yesterday. **00100240**

THE SOUND OF MUSIC • VOLUME 8
10 songs, including: Climb Ev'ry Mountain • Do-Re-Mi • Edelweiss • The Lonely Goatherd • Maria • My Favorite Things • Sixteen Going on Seventeen • So Long, Farewell • Something Good • The Sound of Music. **00100241**

WICKED • VOLUME 9
10 songs, including: As Long as You're Mine • Dancing Through Life • Defying Gravity • For Good • I'm Not That Girl • No One Mourns the Wicked • Popular • What Is This Feeling? • The Wizard and I • Wonderful. **00100242**

LES MISÉRABLES • VOLUME 10
10 songs, including: Bring Him Home • Castle on a Cloud • Do You Hear the People Sing? • Drink with Me (To Days Gone By) • Empty Chairs at Empty Tables • A Heart Full of Love • I Dreamed a Dream • On My Own • Stars • Who Am I?. **00100243**

HAL•LEONARD® CORPORATION

7777 W. BLUEMOUND RD. P.O. BOX 13819 MILWAUKEE, WI 53213

Visit Hal Leonard Online at **www.halleonard.com**

Prices, contents and availability subject to change without notice.

BOOK/CD PACKAGES ONLY $12.95 EACH!

0312